"The art of connecting may have been lost, but Susan McPherson has found it. Her signature question is, How can I help you? Read this book, and she will."

—**Whitney Johnson**, bestselling author of *Build an A-Team*, and LinkedIn 2020 Top Influencer Voice

"*The Lost Art of Connecting* is extraordinary in how it draws a personal blueprint for any personality type—introverts, extroverts, and everyone in between—to build meaningful relationships with their unique set of skills and experiences that will endure and thrive over the course of a lifetime."

—**Alyssa Mastromonaco**, *New York Times* bestselling author and Obama White House Deputy Chief of Staff

"In today's tech-centric world, making meaningful connections really has become something of a lost art. Susan's insightful book is a must-read for anyone looking to put relationships back at the center of business, where they belong."

—**Shelley Zalis**, CEO, The Female Quotient

"Susan McPherson is the living embodiment of the power of connection. Her generosity of spirit and thoughtful introductions have boosted many a career and are the key to her own personal success. Read this book to understand the unique but eminently learnable art of building networks and community and see how much further it takes you."

—**Dee Poku**, founder and CEO, The WIE Suite

"I often hear women entrepreneurs lament, 'I don't have a network, and desperately need one.' Or more specifically, they ask, 'How can I make the connections I need?' *The Lost Art of Connecting* is a must-read for anyone in business, but it is also an essential tool for every aspect of life, no matter your interests and calling. We all need to know how to cultivate relationships, grow our social networks, and build connections that matter. Susan McPherson shows us how and details the rewards. The book is filled with wonderful examples, terrific recommendations, and lots of wisdom. This is one of the best gifts for everyone you know, especially yourself."

—**Melanne Verveer**, former US Ambassador for Global Women's Issues

"Susan McPherson places human connection above all else; she's the ultimate authentic connector—and, lucky us, she's finally sharing how she does it. *The Lost Art of Connecting* is the book we need to get back to the authentic connections we're craving."

—**Tina Wells**, entrepreneur, advisor, author

"Whether you are an executive, an associate, or job seeker, *The Lost Art of Connecting* is the handbook you need to cultivate meaningful relationships. McPherson infuses her guidance with humor, vulnerability, and encouragement. It's a joy to read and will forever change the way you think about networking."

—**Beth Comstock**, author of *Imagine It Forward,* and former Vice Chair, GE

"Guided by a smart framework to offer support rather than asking to receive it, *The Lost Art of Connecting* provides readers a simple but profound paradigm shift for the way you develop strategic relationships in business and in your life."

—Soraya Darabi, General Partner, Trail Mix Ventures

"Susan McPherson is the ultimate authentic connector—and, lucky us, she's finally sharing how she does it. Whether you're a business leader or a movement builder, *The Lost Art of Connecting* is the book we need to get back to the authentic connections we are craving."

—Shannon Watts, founder, Moms Demand Action

"Meaningful connections are the only thing that matters in life. Susan's new book helps you understand how to use technology and authenticity to forge deeper relationships in an increasingly disconnected world. Her real life, practical experience makes this book a truly helpful guide to forging business relationships that go beyond business."

—Jean Oelwang, president and founding CEO, Virgin Unite, and founder of Plus Wonder

"Every business leader knows the value relationships bring to the table, but in our increasingly isolated world of Zoom chats, apps, and platforms, how do we go about building those deep, meaningful relationships that stand the test of time? Serial connector and entrepreneur Susan McPherson shares her secrets on how to do just that in an encouraging, warm, and unique way. *The Lost Art of Connecting* is a must-read."

—Rebecca Minkoff, creative director and founder of Rebecca Minkoff

"Susan reminds us that the happiness we feel and the career success we achieve is dependent on the relationships that we cultivate. *The Lost Art of Connecting* is your roadmap to building deep, meaningful, and timeless relationships that lead to better life outcomes."

—Dan Schawbel, author *of Back to Human, Promote Yourself,* and *Me 2.0*

"Susan McPherson is one of the most connected people I know, and *The Lost Art of Connecting* shares her brilliant strategies. This book will help you not only make more relationships, but also relationships that are more authentic, meaningful, and mutually beneficial. Highly recommended!"

—Lindsey Pollak, *New York Times* bestselling author of *Recalculating*

"Can digital life be as warm as human interaction? Yes, if Susan McPherson is your coach. With her guidance and a new mantra—'How can I help?'—netiquette is transformed into intimacy. If you have zero time, a huge heart, and want to deepen your network, get this book."

—Lisa Stone, cofounder and former CEO of Blogher

"In a digital-first world where in-person gatherings are becoming ever more difficult, Susan McPherson's manifesto on the art of connecting will not only help your career—it just may change your life. Shot through with practical advice, warmth, and Susan's unique approach to building lasting connections, the impact of this book is sure to stay with you."

—**Pat Mitchell**, founder/Editorial Director, TEDWomen, and chair, Sundance Institute Board

"In *The Lost Art of Connecting*, Susan McPherson challenges the old, 'it's who you know' mindset to frame a new world where the depth and quality of relationships are what now differentiate people. It's a must-read for anyone who seeks to cultivate the ultimate competitive advantage in the age of digital transformation: their humanity."

—**Dov Seidman**, founder and Chairman of LRN and The HOW Institute for Society, and the author of *How*

"Having built a career and business based on human connection, I am so excited about the message that Susan shares in *The Lost Art of Connecting*. Human connection is the ignition flame for every successful relationship, business, friendship, and daily interaction—it is what makes us kind, empathetic, and collaborative—it has dimmed lately, and this book will reignite the torch."

—**Jane Wurwand**, founder, Dermalogica and the FOUND initiative

"Throughout my career, I have found the number one ingredient for success is relationships. In the age of social media, it's easy to misinterpret social media engagement as genuine connection. The former is a fleeting metric, and the latter is an indispensable business tool. *The Lost Art of Connecting* shows you that genuine connections are a lifelong asset—and more attainable than you think."

—**Bea Perez**, Senior Vice President and Global Chief of Communications, Sustainability and Strategic Partnerships, The Coca-Cola Company

"There's a difference between a contact and a connection. Susan McPherson is quite good at the latter and will help you figure out how to make the most of every contact and connection you have. Her wisdom is priceless."

—**Abigail E. Disney**, filmmaker/podcaster, philanthropist, and social activist

"In the end, the only thing that matters in this life is your relationships with other people. They're the foundation of happiness, success, and fulfillment and yet they can be so hard to build. So what a gift Susan McPherson has given us with this new book! This is the work of someone who has such a curious mind. Susan explores the barriers that push us apart and prevent us from connecting. But most importantly, she has actionable advice on how people can come together and build the relationships we all desperately need now, more than ever."

—**Carolyn Everson**, Vice President of Global Marketing Solutions, Facebook

"As a seasoned tech executive, and now a six-year entrepreneur, I have experienced many moments of sheer pain running a startup and many moments of ultimate joy. When I reflect on my entrepreneurship journey so far, the moments of true joy are a direct result of me *not* being transactional, spending quality time with the generous and smart people who are *already* in my network, and genuinely asking *how I can help them* with whatever they are working on, with no expectation of anything in return. Invariably, after the interactions where I am 'giving' with a full heart, something great will happen that moves my business forward. Those relationships have lasted for many years and are the dearest to me. Although they started out as 'work connections,' I now know these people's families, and they know mine. This is the whole premise of Susan's brilliant and simple book. I cannot recommend this read enough especially for those who are (a) entrepreneurs or (b) people struggling to make real connections with like-minded humans through the computer screen."

—Karen Cahn, founder and CEO, IFundWomen

"Susan McPherson offers us a delightful and easy to digest guide on how to better connect with one another, and thereby ourselves. This is essential reading for anyone, regardless of the kind of relationship you are seeking, with practical wisdom that is already transforming the way I do business, negotiate, and interact with others. It is the relationship and the value we create for one another that supersedes the superficiality and ephemeral nature of transactional behavior, which as Susan so compassionately teaches, is not connection at all."

—Binta Niambi Brown, founder, oma lilly projects and cofounder, Black Music Action Coalition

"Susan McPherson is the consummate connector, and she has written the ultimate guide to connecting. This is an incredibly timely, absolute must-read for everyone feeling disconnected because of COVID—and not just because of the multitude of practical, easy-to-do recommendations within the 'Gather, Ask, Do' approach. Susan's empathetic and insightful advice will change the way you tackle achieving any goal, in business and in life, for the better."

—Cindy Gallop, consultant and founder/CEO, Make Love Not Porn

"Self-help books are for warm and fuzzy advice, and the business section is for getting things done, right? Wrong. In *The Lost Art of Connecting*, McPherson, one of the most productive women in business today, breaks it down once and for all: you can build meaningful relationships in business and thrive while doing it. Here's your chance to learn from one of the very best!"

—Nathalie Molina Niño, Managing Director, Known Holdings, author of *Leapfrog: The New Revolution for Women Entrepreneurs*

"Susan McPherson is one of the world's great connectors. *The Lost Art of Connecting* is a valuable 'how-to' book filled with nuggets of insight and inspiration along the way."

—Anne-Marie Slaughter, CEO, New America

"There are few people who know how to build meaningful connections like Susan McPherson. She connects purpose and action as an advocate, investor, and in her longtime day job of teaching companies to align their business with broader social progress. But in a time of tech fueled division, racial unrest, and post-pandemic trauma, she is now reminding us how to connect with each other. The fundamental building blocks of life are relationships; in the business world, those relationships are even more vital to addressing the extraordinary challenges we face as a global community—and to getting stuff done with a bit of joy. In her new book, *The Lost Art of Connecting*, McPherson breaks it all down: how to be intentional, authentic, empathetic, inclusive, honest, and effective, without appearing transactional. If you want to change the world, wouldn't it be better to do it together?"

—Ellen McGirt, Senior Editor, *Fortune*

"*The Lost Art of Connecting* upends longstanding transactional 'What can I get out of this?' American business practices, reminding readers that meaningful work starts with meaningful relationships. When you lead with 'How can I help?' as McPherson suggests, you are building the foundation for the kind of relationship that doesn't keep score, but rather allows for the organic unfolding of give, take, and collaborate over the course of a lifetime."

—Pilar Guzmán, writer, editor, cofounder, The Swell

"This topic is more timely than ever. As the global pandemic shuttered us into our caves with only a tech lifeline, it has dawned on us that all those water cooler conversations, happy hours, and company softball games were smart business strategies. Susan McPherson gets us back to basics, helping us rebuild vital relationships to improve both our mental health and our bottom line."

—Dr. Wendy Walsh, "America's Relationship Expert," host of iHeart Media's Dr. Wendy Walsh Show and the podcast Mating Matters

"*The Lost Art of Connecting* is a must-read! Using engaging, relatable stories from her life, Susan McPherson creates a narrative that both informs and guides the reader, and in the process, creates a blueprint for how we can expand our networks to create meaningful connections across all aspects of our lives. With practical tools and a strategy of 'Gather, Ask, Do,' McPherson's book is the inspiration we all need to build connections and then transform them into meaningful relationships that can enrich our lives."

—Jean Case, CEO, Case Impact Network and Chairman, National Geographic Society

THE LOST ART
OF
CONNECTING

THE *GATHER, ASK, DO* METHOD
FOR BUILDING MEANINGFUL BUSINESS
RELATIONSHIPS

SUSAN McPHERSON
with JACKIE ASHTON

New York Chicago San Francisco Athens London Madrid
Mexico City Milan New Delhi Singapore Sydney Toronto

1 2 3 4 5 6 7 8 9   LCR   26 25 24 23 22 21

ISBN   978-1-260-46988-2
MHID   1-260-46988-3

e-ISBN   978-1-260-46989-9
e-MHID   1-260-46989-1

Library of Congress Cataloging-in-Publication Data

Names: McPherson, Susan, author. | Ashton, Jackie (Literary agent), author.
Title: The lost art of connecting : the gather, ask, do method for building meaningful
    business relationships / Susan McPherson with Jackie Ashton.
Description: New York : McGraw-Hill, [2021] | Includes bibliographical references
    and index.
Identifiers: LCCN 2020048444 (print) | LCCN 2020048445 (ebook) |
    ISBN 9781260469882 (hardback) | ISBN 9781260469899 (ebook)
Subjects: LCSH: Business networks. | Business referrals. | Success in business.
Classification: LCC HD69.S8 M38 2021 (print) | LCC HD69.S8 (ebook) |
    DDC 650.1/3—dc23
LC record available at https://lccn.loc.gov/2020048444
LC ebook record available at https://lccn.loc.gov/2020048445

*To my mom, Beryl, who was taken from this earth
far too early, but instilled in me the goodness,
strength, hope, and pragmatism that propelled me
into living a life filled with meaningful relationships
and the pure joy of connecting others.*

CONTENTS

CONTENTS

PART III
DO

INTRODUCTION

Connection is my superpower. It has always come as naturally to me as breathing. I've been called the Serial Connector, a human customer relationship management (CRM) app—and I've spent the last 30 years of my career building relationships that are deep and expansive, spanning decades, even continents. People often ask me: How do you build relationships so easily? Well, connecting—as I've come to understand it—comes down to one simple question: *How can I help?* Asking this question in any meeting, any introduction—any moment—immediately narrows my focus on how I can be of service and support to others.

And isn't that what makes relationships feel meaningful?

Every single person is an introduction to something else: another person, a unique skill, a new project, or something you inevitably will learn about yourself.

It should never be about, *What will I get from this person?*

But instead, *What can I learn? What can I discover?*

Or, *Who could I connect this person with?*

I've always enjoyed threading people together to create something bigger and unknown—the way small children do with those little black circles in dot-to-dot drawings, never certain what the larger picture will be until the final connections are filled in. This method has led me to a career with deep fulfillment and enjoyment. It's connected me to people from all walks of life. It's taken me around the world, given me seats on boards, and introduced me to a lifetime of relationships, experiences, and right here, to you.

Now you and I are connected, too.

"Don't wait until you need a favor to do one for someone else," my father used to say. Most often, he said it from our breakfast table, over eggs and coffee, where my two older siblings and I would vie for elbow room as our parents spent hours poring over as many as six different print newspapers. I grew up in upstate New York—a town 20 minutes north of Albany to be exact—where my parents would start each day at the small wooden kitchen table in our 1,200-square-foot home, among scattered, open pages from day-old copies of the *New York Times,* the *Schenectady Gazette,* the *Albany Times Union,* the *Troy Record,* the local Jewish paper, and the *Boston Globe.* My parents were first generation born in the United States. Their parents came from the old country, specifically Ukraine and Hungary. My mother was an ambitious housewife who managed to do all the things expected of a wife and a mother at the time *and* maintain a vibrant and purposeful life outside the home as a broadcast public relations maven. She would cut out snippets of interesting stories to send to colleagues, family members, or friends, sometimes with a long letter attached. My father, a professor of Russian history at Russell Sage College, would do the same for his students and former students, department members, and other connections, sometimes with a short note that said, "thinking of you," always written with his manual typewriter. His letters were legendary. Their recipients often spanned multiple generations of women he'd taught in one family.

I can still smell the scent of the ink ribbon, hear the click-clack of his typing, the *ping* just before the carriage reached the end of the page. I can hear the slap of my mother's hand atop her stack of addressed envelopes as she patted them, ready to send off that day's batch of greetings—and off they would go. My parents' way of connecting was indeed an art. One that not only brought them personal joy but also career fulfillment, success, and satisfaction.

I watched. And I learned.

WHAT IS A MEANINGFUL BUSINESS RELATIONSHIP?

What makes a relationship meaningful? Many if not most people *expect* to develop meaningful relationships in love, in family, and in friendship—but in business? Aren't you supposed to be tough as nails, even cutthroat? What does a "meaningful relationship" in business even look like? Well, for starters, I've long taken the approach that "work Susan" and "after work Susan" are one and the same person. I've never seen work and life as separate, no doubt because of the way I was raised. A relationship is a *relationship*—whether it's built through business conducted across the boardroom table or over a meal shared at my kitchen table.

But what makes relationships meaningful? For me, the most meaningful relationships are those I've built over the years through my work supporting women, lifting up the voices of those without power, and making the world a better place—using business, community, and investing as a force for positive change in the world. In the pages that follow, I reveal insights I've learned not only from my own art of connecting, but also those I've gleaned through relationships and interviews with dozens of community builders, movement starters, and entrepreneurs as well as psychologists, researchers, and activists. The common thread we all agree on is that to even *begin* to figure out how to go about building meaningful relationships with others, you first need to figure out that all-too-important relationship with yourself.

What's important to *you*? What does *meaningful* even mean to you? Have you ever even stopped to think about it? What is meaningful to you may be different than what's meaningful to me or what's meaningful to someone else—and that's perfectly fine. *Authenticity* has become so much of a buzzword that it borders on meaningless these days. But to build *meaningful* relationships you don't need to connect with the 8 billion people on this planet. In fact, you shouldn't. What I hope to share in the pages of this book is: first, how to define what meaningful means to you; second, how to seek others who not only share your values and your vision but also those who challenge you, expose your blind spots, and broaden the diversity and breadth of your network; and third, of course, how to make those relationships deep and rewarding.

And that is the art of connecting.

But first I ask you to define what makes a relationship meaningful to you. Take a sheet of paper and write down the answer. Then add your response to this: What are the top three most meaningful business relationships you've had in your life and what made them so?

Your answers here are important as they will guide you toward *your* constellation.

WHAT MOST PEOPLE GET WRONG ABOUT BUSINESS RELATIONSHIPS

Business relationships often get a bad reputation for being too "transactional," and for good reason. To most people, a new LinkedIn contact or a coveted introduction sounds off an internal monologue: *What can this person do for me?* And that is why I was motivated to write this book. I see so many people today going about connection all wrong. Most people are so busy working *for* people that they fail to work *with* them, developing positive relationships through a thousand small touchpoints. They are adding more and more contacts, attending a zillion events, slogging through endless Zoom calls, and wondering why they feel depleted and lonely at the end of a long day. But in my eyes, people don't stand alone. They aren't a small isolated "dot," but are instead an instrumental piece in something much more extensive, a part of a grander vision. *People* do business with *people*. And when you make a genuine connection, it sparks learning and knowledge sharing, reduces burnout, spurs innovation, and creates a sense of purpose and well-being, too. I love facilitating introductions and bringing people together in a myriad of ways.

But I'm the exception, not the norm.

Most people today feel *disconnected*.

Between the years 1985 and 2009, the average American's social network *shrank*, meaning their number of close confidants declined by up to one-third.[1] This is true for both the young and the old.[2] We're living in a loneliness epidemic that is causing declines in physical and mental health, as well as decreased work satisfaction and performance.[3, 4] Now on top of that, as I write these pages, the world is in the midst of the coronavirus pandemic that has forced people to self-isolate and physically stay apart. It's clear that the art of connecting is indeed lost. We're talking, Zooming, Tweeting, and texting, but we're not feeling a sense of connection. People have lost their sense of belonging and purpose in their careers and their lives. Why? Because we've come to lean too hard on our digital lives. Virtual connections are not the end; they are the *means* to an end—an authentic relationship with depth, be it professional or personal. And that is what this book is all about: how to build that all-elusive depth.

Now for the next question: What is missing in your business relationships today? In other words: Why did you buy this book? Write your answer down underneath your answers from earlier. Now you are starting to home in on what will best serve you in each of the *Gather*, *Ask*, *Do* phases of my method.

START WITH THE "I"
IN HOW CAN I HELP?

Any meaningful relationship starts with you—your vulnerable, real self. And therein lies the reason depth escapes us: we have to be flawed, we have to be real, we have to be human. What we want to be is perfect, successful, flawless—especially at work!

But that doesn't inspire real connection.

But before we even get there, to that scary, real, vulnerable place—start with what you need. Who do you need around you to be your best? What are your unique values and strengths? What are the most urgent and pressing problems of the world, and how can *you* (and only you) make your unique contribution to solve them?

The answers to these questions will point you toward who you want to be connected with to best fulfill your career and life's purpose. And when you find *that*—magic can transpire.

Once you get good at building meaningful connections, you can facilitate them for others as well, amplifying the effect. The truth is that whether or not a connection is meaningful honestly has very little to do with the other person. Feeling lonely, isolated, or disconnected is an inside job. How connected you feel is determined by the meaning that *you* ascribe to that relationship.[5] It's subjective: How do *I feel* about this relationship? You can be in a crowd full of 200 people and feel abysmally lonely. Or you can be seated at a dinner table with your closest confidant and feel that way, too. Or you can be curled up on the sofa with only your rescue pup (I am with my partner in crime, Phoebe, as I write these words) and feel deeply fulfilled and connected. The difference between feeling alone and *happy* versus alone and *lonely* comes down to expectations. When you desire solitude, being alone feels wonderful! But when you are alone and wish to be with others (or when you are with others among whom you don't feel comfortable), loneliness can arise.

Connection is determined by how it feels to *you*.

In this book, I will share the tips and tricks I've learned over my long and fruitful career connecting with thousands, facilitating connections between others, and watching others do so, too. My mother used to always tell me, "Meet boys so you can meet their friends." And the same is true in business—you should meet people so you can meet the people they know and admire. But I like to take my mother's advice one step further, asking not who you *want* to meet, but who you *need* to meet. Who are the people who will best compliment your strengths and help you be your best self? Who are the people who could most benefit from your assets and knowledge? What exposure to people of different racial, gender, and other backgrounds do you lack? Where do you need to be pushed outside of your comfort zone?

And the best way I've found to find and build these relationships always comes back to that one key question: *How can I help?*

A NEW APPROACH TO BUILDING MEANINGFUL CONNECTIONS

When I talk about how to build meaningful connections, I use the illustration of a constellation. There are 250 billion stars in the galaxy. Not all of them align in just the right way to make that special sight that is the constellation. And like networking, you never know just how you are connected to another person until you put in the work to see the patterns. I've broken down my method for creating your personal network of stars, for creating magic in relationships by asking "How can I help?" I call it the *Gather, Ask, Do* method. This method will not only help you create *your* constellation, but it will give you the tools to help others create constellations, too—many of them. And that is perhaps the most rewarding aspect of this method: not only the deeply nourishing relationships that you will develop, but also the ripple effect of connecting others. The brightly lit constellations that you will see among others. In the *Gather* stage, you will learn how to better connect with yourself, defining your business values and goals, and determine how you can help and whom, and who would help you grow. In the *Ask* phase, you will continue to ask "How can I help," as well as deepening your relationships by asking more and more questions, building the depth of your connections and curiosity. In the *Do* phase of my approach, you will take action—immediately doing the helping in all the ways that you possibly can, building trust, competence, and depth of connections. Because the most magic in our relationships happens when we truly *see* and *are seen* by the people we're connecting with.

Recent research reveals that people with a robust social network of confidants have better job performance, feel more fulfilled, and even live longer.[6] But my parents didn't need a peer-reviewed study to tell them that. They understood the *art of connecting*. Indeed, my parents were the epitome of connection, the original social media influencers, growing their "following" with each clipping sent, each scoop of slightly spiked punch (we had no budget for cocktails), and each thank-you card written—all while remaining completely authentic in the process. They tended to their network like a garden, watering, freshening the soil, pruning old leaves, taking care. Their effort reaped tremendous depth, so unlike our current "follow back" culture that has divided us in an ever-growing list of ways.

Today, I use our exploding communication tools to bring people together from different sectors in ways that were never possible before, and without any of the antagonism or competition that makes networking feel like a dirty word. Instead, I nurture and bring people together, rather than pitting them against one another to see who wins the Twitter showdown. Whether it's a former boss on the West Coast, a best friend from my hometown, or the high school student I met at a friend's child's graduation wanting to know more about my business, they're all part of that same constellation. This approach for seeing, making space for, and acting on potential connections has allowed me to fuse my life and my work without burnout, overwhelm, or anxiety.

This book will show you how I've done that, give you the tools to use the art of connecting, and create the constellation of people you need to bring your life's work to fruition.

PART I

GATHER

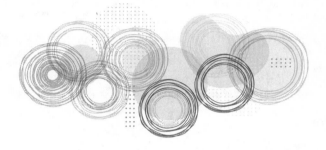

FOCUS: How do you create the conditions for relationships to flourish in your office—whether it's physical or virtual—and among potential partners? Refocus the goals of traditional networking by prioritizing what's in front of you: who you know, your current skills, and existing contacts. Do not underestimate the power of connections unrelated to your business plan. Reach out to your current network and zoom in on the challenges they face: How can you help or support? By doing so, you will make yourself an invaluable asset, a trusted resource for others that will far outlast the gains from a quick LinkedIn follow. In this section, you will learn how to gather the stars of your constellation by first examining your relationship with yourself and clarifying your goals. Then you will learn several tips and strategies to begin to expand your network of connections in ways that feel natural and inspiring, and don't zap your energy.

HELP, I DON'T KNOW ANYONE!

We've all been there: a networking event, the first day at a new job, or even just a big meeting. We walk into the room and—*panic sets in*—I don't know these people! It even happens to extroverts like me.

Growing up with parents who were serial connectors—long before that was an expression—I just assumed everyone was like them. Boy, was I wrong. A lot of people *think* about connecting. But few act on it. Especially today.

There are ever more ways to connect, but there are exactly as many ways to disconnect. I've found that in all cases people fail to maintain the right mindset about connecting. No matter the location, the specifics of the meeting, or who is there, people are full of excuses *not* to connect.

Here's an excuse I hear all the time: "I can't move forward with my career goals because I don't know the right people." This is far from the case. Every *single* person you know—regardless of their experience or background—can help you in some way. With a simple mindset reboot, you can drastically improve your ability to build business relationships. The philosopher William James said, "If you can change your mind, you can change your life." And in this chapter, my goal is to change your mind about networking. *Don't discount the possibilities in your current network.* Start there and you will reap enormous rewards from what is right in front of you.

CONNECT WITH YOURSELF

First and foremost, connect with yourself. Are you an extrovert who loves gatherings and people, and derives energy from others? Or are you someone who prefers intimate gatherings and getting together less frequently? Knowing this about yourself is key to implementing the art of connecting in a sustainable way. When you stay intentional, you make the biggest impact—connecting and communicating with people without burnout or fatigue.

Esther Perel is a renowned psychotherapist and the bestselling author of *Mating in Captivity*. On her podcast *How's Work?* Perel examines how the skill of navigating relationships isn't something that differs much between the home and the office. Perel says that the narratives people develop from their childhood and family of origin—even though most people aren't entirely aware of this—can spill over into their careers. How we handle conflict, how we communicate, the way we develop trust—these are all skills that we tend to develop as children and can't really escape when we walk into "work." So it's worth asking yourself: How were meaningful relationships built in your past? In your family? Simply taking a look at that and being open to the idea that our "work self" and "personal self" might be the same can teach you a lot about your relational skills (or deficits!) and what you might need to focus on or build to deepen the relationships in your work life. It might seem like "connecting with yourself" is something you do *after* work, but doing so in a business setting is essential.

Other expert connectors and relationship builders I spoke to agreed. Jamia Wilson is the executive editor and publisher of the Feminist Press. She also recommends that before reaching out to make connections, we become reacquainted with ourselves. Wilson pointed out to me that sometimes we are so focused on "getting things done"—striving for goals and deliverables all while managing the bills and the mortgage—that we forget who we are. And when we're not deeply connected to who we are and what we stand for— we can lose sight of the best path for our connections. She told me:

> When I make efforts to be gentle and compassionate enough to get to know myself—all of it, good, bad, and perfectly imperfect—then I can be an open person to listen and hear and connect with others.

She added that this frees her from feeling confined by what society needs her to do, and she can be more open to others. As an example of this, she pointed out that nature and the animal kingdom are brilliant at staying connected to their intention—their why of being. A lion doesn't forget that he's king of the jungle because he's burned out, but as human beings, sometimes we veer off course and need to come back to ourselves. She also points out that it's absolutely okay to have interactions that feel awkward. We can learn from each of those interactions and do better next time. Instead of thinking *Oh, maybe that rubbed that person the wrong way* or *I'm not sure if I fit in with this group*, it's more helpful to think: *What did that interaction teach me about myself? What can I create from that?*

When you remind yourself who you really are and what you really want—you're far better set up to connect with those who will align with your goals. And you will be far less likely to fail in business relationships because you've resorted to what is often called "spray and pray"—where you just spew your messages out into the ether and hope someone grabs onto what you are saying. Be intentional: know who you are and know what you want, and you will attract those who can help you.

START WITH WHO YOU KNOW

Oftentimes in networking, we get pigeonholed into reaching out to specific people. But in reality, someone who is already in your immediate network might be able to introduce you to the correct person. One of the most powerful changes you can make right away to improve your business relationships is to change your mindset. *Your existing network is your biggest asset—use it.*

Sure, you might not have a direct contact to *the* bigwig investor you'd like to pitch to, but someone in your immediate network might. They might be your best friend's uncle, your yoga instructor's nephew, or your hairdresser's cousin. It sounds painfully obvious, but so few people act on this simple strategy: *reach out to every existing connection.* The rebuttal I usually hear is, "But they aren't the *right* person." It doesn't matter! That person has contacts, friends, and relatives. Better yet, they have something to teach you—guaranteed—whether they are an intern, a CEO, or a car attendant for the parking lot. Every *single* person has something to offer that can enrich your career and by extension, your life. And you, in turn, have something to offer them.

The other mistake I see? A million excuses for failing to connect: I'm too busy, she's too senior, he's not senior enough, they don't have the right experience, and on and on. If you're fresh out of college, you might think, what could I possibly offer a CEO? But recent grads have a wealth of information; they are the front lines of emerging trends and technology. For many companies, they are target customers. Think you're too young (or too new to your industry) and don't know anything? Think again. Maybe your contact's company is launching in a city you know well—you could offer free market research. Successful people know that inspiration and learning from disparate sources and types of people can serve you well. The possibilities are endless.

Usually the hang-up is in our heads. (Especially for women, who have been socialized to talk themselves out of new connections by saying "Oh, I don't want to bother that person.") So we need to get out of our heads. No one is off limits, and if you think you have nothing to offer them, or they have nothing to offer you—then you are leaving a wealth of information, connections, synergies, learning, and growth (and happiness!) on the table. I also find that in most cases, when people throw out the excuse that they don't want to "bother" someone else, it's usually an excuse to avoid vulnerability—the very thing that can allow a meaningful connection to transpire. The next time you find yourself canceling a connection because that person feels out of reach or you don't want to "put them out," pause to consider whether the real obstacle might be fear. Fear of rejection, fear of closeness, fear of failure, or even just fear of feeling awkward.

"Who you know" includes your colleagues, coworkers, and office mates, too. How well do you know the people you work with? How much of an effort have you made to have a genuine, quality relationship with the people you do business with each day? Connectivity across the organization and across networks not only feels good, it also spurs creativity. A study published in the *Journal of Applied Psychology* found that the cross-fertilization of ideas among the people in your direct network offers a creative boost and can even have an impact up to the third and fourth degree.[1] That's a pretty remarkable finding: idea sharing and collaboration have a ripple effect that can positively impact people in ways you may never know about. A new connection can lead to a new partner, a new colleague, or an innovative idea. It could even lead to an entire new community of people to broaden your knowledge base, boost your creativity, and lead to something unexpected.

Another excuse? Introversion or shyness. It's true that some people, like my parents, were natural connectors; they made new connections with ease. Research about the evolutionary components of social networks shows that some of the ability to create a currency of social capital is embedded in our genes.[2] Some human beings have a natural ability to make friends, to engage in conversation, and to reveal their humanity in a way that encourages friendship. But if you're not an extrovert, or if you cringe at the idea of schmoozing and networking, fret not. Like anything, the art of gathering connections is a learned skill, too. And the tools revealed in this book will highlight ways to expand your social fabric without anxiety.

CLARIFY YOUR GOAL

The next step is to clarify your goals. And here's where we start to zoom in on that "connect with yourself" mindset: What do you want to accomplish in your career and in your life? An important distinction: this is not the goal of your meeting or even necessarily the subject of your initial conversation. Right now, clarifying your business goals is for *you* to get clear in your objectives. (The goal of the meeting is to establish or deepen a long-term, reciprocal relationship—but more on that later.)

For now, what do you want to achieve: Are you looking for a new job or promotion? Launching a new business? Looking for a donor or funder? Whatever the case may be, make this very clear and *write it down*. Most people think about their goals. Successful people write them down. But the ultra-successful? They write them down and recognize that goals may be short term, but relationships are long term. When you clarify your goals, the constellation to which you'd like to belong emerges into view.

Most people, even some very successful ones, take a "me, me, me" approach to business relationships, which is incredibly short-sighted. Just by avoiding this pitfall, you will set yourself apart. Set goals to get clear about what you want and how to make the best use of your time and relationships so that you don't waste anyone's time. Never approach a connection with the intention of "getting something" from them.

Write down your business goal and then make a list of the top connections that you have whom you could learn from or help. Don't leave anyone off because of fear-based ("I don't want them to feel burdened" or "They wouldn't be interested") or closed-minded ("They're too young/old/experienced/inexperienced") thinking.

CONNECT TO LISTEN, LEARN, AND HELP

Today, when we think of "building a network," we tend to think of technology: LinkedIn, Twitter, Instagram, Facebook. These are brilliant tools that many of us use daily, often to significant effect. But the key is going *beyond the transactional*—the accepted friend request, the like, the retweet, the favor, or the forward. As we will explore throughout this book, relationships we cultivate with depth can impact our health and our career in unexpected ways. So here's my challenge to you: before you send that LinkedIn request or write out that email to the person you want to connect with, brainstorm two or three ideas for ways that you could help them. Are they working on a project you know something about? Are they launching in a city you know well? Are they raising awareness for a cause that you could showcase on your social platforms? Most people will go into a coffee, lunch, or meeting laser-focused on what they can *get* from it. As I was writing this chapter, I received about 20 requests in my inbox, as I typically do. But imagine the response your email will get when instead of an email that includes a dreaded "Can I pick your brain" request, the recipient instead reads something like, "I see you're opening an office in Atlanta, where I grew up—I'd love to help connect you with the people I know there. Can we meet for coffee?"

I bet you're already feeling more at ease about setting up these types of meetings, aren't you? When you eliminate the "what can I get?" or "how can I impress them?" from the equation, there's no anxiety. When you go with the intent of *learning* and *offering,* the focus is on them and not you. You will then find yourself with a deeper relationship, and it's quite likely that your favor will be returned or a real friendship will emerge.

When you meet with someone, set a goal to understand *their* world and their circumstances, offer to help *them* with something they need, or invite them to something you both enjoy doing to foster a deeper connection that can help you in the future. It completely levels the playing field and makes everyone far more comfortable and open. If you can connect as a human (are you both middle children? love to travel? interested in environmental causes?), then you will have a cheerleader in your corner who can serve both of you in synergistic ways. This could be the beginning of a constellation.

Perhaps you're not even the best contact for this person, but you could connect them with others who are. Connect with them on a human level: Where are they from? What is their family, heritage, or culture like? Knowing those details creates meaningful conversation. It creates the threads from which the ties of connection can be made. If you only talk about work, then you miss the underlying attributes that make us human—our shared commonalties and who we truly are.

Connecting as humans sounds like such straightforward advice to the point of being absurdly obvious—but research shows that this is a skill we've forgotten. A recent Cigna survey revealed that 46 percent of adults in the United States sometimes feel alone, and 54 percent said they always or sometimes feel that no one knows them well.[3] Think about that for a moment: over half of the people in this country feel as though *no one* knows them. That is a staggering statistic. Not only is this bad for business, as people do business with people, but research shows that lonely feelings can take years off our lives. One study found that lonely people have a 26 percent higher risk of dying.[4] Loneliness produces the stress hormone cortisol, which can lead to high blood pressure, increased inflammation, and a depressed immune system. And contrary to the common association between getting older and feeling alone, surprisingly, Gen Z (ages 18 to 22) and Millennials (ages 23 to 37) score the highest on the loneliness scale.[5] In contrast, research shows that a deep, authentic social network can add up to 15 years to your life. But most of us are so busy trying to do our jobs, pay the bills, and accomplish more, more, more that we end up depleted at the end of the day, and our connections with others feel just as empty as we feel inside. If you simply make it a daily practice to listen, learn, and help each time you connect with someone, you will notice an instant change in how fulfilled you feel. And remember that at the end of the day, we are all human and all human beings speak the same emotional language.

When I was in kindergarten, we lived in Romania while my dad completed a Fulbright scholarship as a visiting professor at the University of Bucharest. I was surrounded by children speaking

Romanian—a Balkan romance language that sounds a bit like German, French, English, Greek, Slavic, and Hungarian all blended into one. I couldn't really understand a word the kids around me were saying. But somehow, I connected with them on a human level. A five-year-old is a five-year-old, no matter where they were born. Instead of staying rigid, clinging to their differences, kids tend to have a way of zooming in on their similarities. Their eyes know how to say, "Meet me at the swing set?" (Except at that time, there were only makeshift swings in Romania.) We may not have spoken the same language, but I still managed to teach them how to jump rope!

You don't need to speak the same language to connect. I've always been able to form bonds with lots of different people from diverse industries, continents, and walks of life, and I trace some of it back to those early days in southeastern Europe. We lived among the Romanian people and not like dignitaries who were with the US Department of State. If we wanted a chicken at dinner, our neighbor upstairs would have to take its head off and remove the feathers. Those days in Romania showed me that openness, curiosity, and inquisitiveness are the essential building blocks of connection and trust, laying the foundation for building a vast network of differing personalities, talents, and interests.

I often say, "We have two ears and one mouth for a reason." It's always a good idea to stay open-minded, intellectually curious, and inquisitive. Though sometimes we resist making in-person connections—especially with people we don't know very well—it's good for your brain to be social. A 2011 study revealed how the neurobiological endogenous opioid system (our body's innate, internal pain-relieving system) plays a role in positive social interactions.[6] Positively interacting with other humans lights up the part of the brain that makes us feel good. It is a natural high with no side effects. No matter how uncomfortable or nerve-racking an in-person meeting or gathering might seem, it is contributing valuable real estate to your life's community. And more often than not, it creates healthy feel-good sensations in our brain, too.

Of course, my father didn't need to read a clinical study to understand the benefit of personal connections. He just knew. "Oh, Susan," he would say, "you're going to Boston, you need to look up your third cousin Leonard." Spinning an ever-growing web of connection was etched into the fiber of my being.

BUILD LONG-TERM RELATIONSHIPS, AND DON'T SEPARATE "WORK"

My parents were blind to the differences between coworkers, neighbors, friends, or family—people were people. Each one was worthy of connection, depth, and care. Each one was a human, someone who could add breadth and vitality to their network, regardless of *how* they met. Before she rejoined the workforce full bore when I was in the second grade, my mother used to host an annual, meticulously planned open house for my father's history department and college colleagues, which took her a full three months to prepare. She arranged everything from the cream cheese and smoked salmon sandwiches shaped into rounds, stars, and squares using cookie cutters, to the arrival of the guests, which she staggered to arrive in overlapping timeframes (4 to 6 p.m., 5 to 7 p.m., and 6 to 8 p.m.) to allow a steady rotation of old and new faces. Above all, she made it her mission to create an environment where people were comfortable connecting.

But most people don't see their acquaintances in the same way. According to a study conducted by Olivet Nazarene University, Americans, on average, recognize only 15 percent of their coworkers as "real friends."[7] Forty-one percent are just coworkers, and 22 percent are strangers.[8] (*Strangers*—no wonder people feel lonely.) There's a sense that we have to keep our guard up at the office, to not appear weak or vulnerable. But I advocate for *developing real friendships at work*. You don't have to wait to become friends with a colleague, and you never know where these friendships can lead.

Take, for example, my relationship with Madeline Jennings, a former executive who helped me secure my first "real" job as a researcher at *USA Today*. She was on the board of trustees at the college my father taught at (remember how my parents made no distinction between friend and colleague?) and I met her through him. Thirty years later, we are still in touch. I still send her notes and letters, and she sends me postcards on her trips and journeys. She now is in her 80s, and she recently introduced me to her niece who lived near me in Brooklyn, who I recruited to join a nonprofit where I held a board seat. This is the perpetuation of the personal connection; it's a real friendship. If you are vulnerable and your authentic self, you are much more likely to make connections. We're all human and all humans have vulnerabilities. What could have been a passing acquaintance or a short-term relationship instead becomes friends for life. Viewing a new contact as a lifelong relationship also takes the pressure off of each individual event or meeting—each one is a building block, a step toward a rich and deep connection designed to last and bear fruit for both of you. Each note, card, conversation, and coffee is a touchpoint that deepens that connection over time.

Rob Cross is a professor of business at Babson College, and he has studied the impact of cultivating social networks for almost 20 years. And his research also backs up what my parents (especially my mother) knew: The people who are the happiest in their careers have *real friends at work*.[9] Cross discovered that people who take the time to cultivate nourishing relationships are more likely to feel fulfilled—even if they work a mundane or stressful job. Think intimacy, vulnerability, and friendship have no place at work? Think again: trust, listening, open exchange of ideas, and feedback—these are all elements that spring from intimacy. Developing a feeling of mutual closeness with people doesn't always happen quickly; it takes time to cultivate, one envelope (or Tweet) at a time. But I firmly believe you can dive right in and make it clear that your intention is to become friends. And whether you're retweeting or writing by hand to cultivate the relationship—it's not the medium that matters so much as the intention, the frequency, and the content. It's the *action*, not the thought, that counts.

My mother knew inherently that connection with other people feeds the soul, and science backs this up—there is a plethora of research now that shows the role that dopamine, serotonin, oxytocin, and other "feel-good chemicals" in the brain are connected to positive social interaction.[10] She also knew that having a successful career is as much a matter of relationships, personal and professional, as it is the work itself. Cross's research has shown that thriving—being at the top of your game in terms of your well-being—doesn't have anything to do with the actual specifics of your work, believe it or not. It's not dependent on your role or the amount of stress you feel, or the demands of your job. Instead, he found that it has everything to do with the quality and depth of your relationships, how you engage and interact with the people in your workplace, and even those in your personal life. This is an important finding to take into consideration the next time you're feeling burnout, stress, or job dissatisfaction. When you're feeling overwhelmed at work, maybe what you need isn't less—or different—work, but better relationships.

VOLUNTEER OR JOIN CAUSES LOCALLY

Although we have lots of new tools to gather today, I still advise young people who are starting off in a new place to get involved in organizations they care about. It's a strategy that's served me again and again, particularly when I faced the biggest tragedy of my life.

In December 1986, I was 22 years old working toward a masters in broadcast journalism at Boston University. Thanks to my mother's connections, I'd secured a job in Washington, DC, over the break at the National Association of Broadcasters. As I was driving back from a New Year's date with my boyfriend, I received news that would forever change my life. My mother, then 56, had died on New Year's Eve in a fire at the Dupont Plaza Hotel in San Juan, Puerto Rico, while on vacation with my father. A hotel employee, angry over a labor dispute with the hotel ownership, set on fire the fuel in a storage room, igniting a raging inferno that quickly burned out of control, killing 97 people and injuring hundreds more. My parents were not staying in the hotel. My dad had merely dropped my mom off so she could enjoy a guilty pleasure, playing the slot machines. Tragically, the last time he saw her was 30 minutes before the fire was set.

For days, weeks, months, and even years, I was engulfed in shock, wrecked with pure devastation, and enraged by the utter disregard for humanity. I couldn't believe it. Here today, gone tomorrow.

Three years after my mother's death, and two years after a devastating breakup, I moved from Washington, DC, to Newport Beach in Southern California, for a job in marketing at *USA Today*. Leaving behind everyone and everything I knew, I had to start building a community from scratch. When I landed in Newport Beach—missing my mother and desperate to replace my grief with new feelings of connection, purpose, and productivity—I started volunteering and working with nonprofits. When you roll up your sleeves to work on issues you care about, you're sure to meet likeminded people who share your values. You build relationships that can reap untold rewards. I didn't have access to any of the communication tools we love to hate today. So instead of connecting with friends on Facebook, colleagues on LinkedIn, or joining a Meetup, I opened the yellow pages and got involved with all the nonprofits I could, to build a real-life "following" on the West Coast. I'd eventually hold dinner parties of my own, though on a much smaller scale than my mother's. And piece by piece, I cobbled together a community, a career, and a life that still feeds me to this day.

When you start over in a new town or new industry, the reach and impact of your network, however small it may feel, may surprise you. Imagine that you move to a new town as I did, and after a few days there, you know only four people. Your local network is four, right? Wrong. For each of those four people you've made a connection with, you're now connected to their friends (your second-degree network), and their friends (your third-degree network), and their friends (your fourth-degree network). Research shows that you can (in some instances, such as with voting and eating habits, as well as happiness) be influenced by the people you're linked to with up to four degrees of separation.[11] So although you may feel as if you are connected to only four individual people in this example, you are in fact impacted by hundreds if not thousands more. Nicholas Christakis is a sociologist and physician known for his research on social networks and the socioeconomic, biosocial, and evolutionary determinants of human behavior and longevity. In his popular TED Talk, he shares captivating tales about the hidden influence of social networks. Christakis has uncovered surprising findings about happiness and altruism and has proven that human beings are in fact interconnected to hundreds or even thousands of other people, most of whom we do not know.

PRIORITIZE CONNECTORS

I also recommend that you prioritize establishing connections with connectors, especially if they are your boss. Part of the art of connecting is not only recognizing how to connect with others, but also realizing who can *complement* you in a variety of areas. When it comes to the workplace, there are myriad benefits bestowed upon connectors, especially when it comes to management. Of the four different types of managers (teachers, cheerleaders, always-on, and connectors), connectors are the most successful.[12] Teachers are those managers who, just as the name confers, make a point of giving you instructions on everything you need to do your job well. Cheerleaders, in contrast, will support and encourage you, leading you from afar and guiding you to, in most cases, figure things out on your own. An always-on manager is one who is available at any time to provide what you might need—to answer questions, give feedback, or just listen. But a connector manager is one who uses their network, whether it's with another team member, a partner, or a customer, to expand the breadth and depth of the teachers you have at your disposal. A connector manager realizes that they may have the expertise you need in some areas, but that for others, a different person could better teach you that skill. It makes sense in terms of efficiency ("It's better for Bob to teach you how to code"), building trust ("I don't need to overmanage you or pretend I know everything"), as well as communication. Jaime Roca and Sari Wilde, authors of *The Connected Manager: Why Some Leaders Build Exceptional Talent—and Others Don't*, found that of the four different types of leaders, connector managers build the strongest and most effective teams. Working for a connector manager triples the likelihood that direct reports will be high performers, and doing so boosts employee engagement by up to 40 percent. It makes sense from a productivity perspective; connector managers seem to distribute effort and work in a way that is efficient for all. Plus, when you're on the receiving end of a connection, it gives you a positive feeling. Making a connection requires noticing, and paying attention. And when your manager pays attention to you and *sees* you, it feels good.

PRECONNECT

Even if you dislike big groups, a conference or large-scale event will inevitably land on your calendar. You might find yourself one hour before the event thinking, *I'd rather not.* You're not alone. *We're all fricking terrified.* If getting together in a big group feels frightening, try your best to instead attend or create smaller, more intimate gatherings. In fact, this is what I like to do most often today. I enjoy and recommend bringing small groups of people together who can learn from each other and when you do that, the network itself strengthens. This is also why I'm such a big supporter of social clubs and rely heavily on curated gatherings for my work today. It's in these spaces where innovative, cross-industry connections that otherwise wouldn't be possible inside an office building can be made. Technology also has a prominent place here, since when we go down Internet rabbit holes and find people online who share our values, social media becomes a means to spread good instead of anger. As our living and working situations grow more fragmented, having other people on your team at your fingertips couldn't be more valuable.

But in those instances in which a conference or large gathering appears on your agenda, I recommend facilitating an introduction or even preconnecting. Many conferences and summits provide an app and encourage you to connect using it ahead of the opening day. Here you can find people who are also attending that event who share common interests with you. Send them a note and say something like, "I'll be there Friday, but I don't know many people. Want to grab a coffee after the morning session, and talk about ocean conservation?" This takes away the pressure of having to make a connection in-person and helps take some of the anxiety away. The same preconnection step helps when I am introducing people, too. If I can help start a conversation or point out a common interest or skill people have, it goes so much more smoothly and helps everyone feel comfortable. I do this at my parties, with our clients, as well as with my team. Use Google, Instagram, or LinkedIn to help you find a conversation starter. Even if you don't make plans to meet face-to-face before or at the event, simply having an email exchange helps each of you make the other person's acquaintance. But here is where most people fall into the "avoid discomfort" trap: don't let the tool take over the relationship itself, but rather use it as a tool for *kickstarting* the relationship. Lean on technology in the getting-to-know-you phase, but don't use it as a crutch for avoiding face-to-face relationships. If you've been LinkedIn, email, or What's App corresponding with someone for quite some time and haven't yet taken the relationship offline, this is a perfect opportunity to take a relationship from casual to meaningful with an in-person conversation.

THE BOTTOM LINE

Even if you're just starting out in a new job, a new city, or a new industry, you know far more people than you realize. Don't limit your work connections to those people within the walls of your business. Your existing networks can be used to great effect—often there are connections hiding in places you won't expect, and there are relationships to be built in places you would have never imagined.

The more people you know, and the better you know them, the more likely you are to succeed. And if you've worked hard to *help* those people, then you can be certain that those favors will come back your way, tenfold.

To need connection is human. But to get it—that is the key to life.

INVITE TO GET INVITED

Networking in the traditional sense has somehow become synonymous with *hustling*—get out there, meet people, press palms. When I think of a networking event, I envision a woman standing in an elevator. She's about to walk into a hotel ballroom filled with people she doesn't know. She wears her best suit; her pockets are filled with business cards. Though she looks polished and ready to greet on the outside, inside she is thinking to herself, "God, I just want to go upstairs and order room service." This is "net *working*"— it sounds like and often feels like a chore. Instead, let's call it helping or creating a constellation—doesn't that sound more rewarding?

Traditional networking is typically motivated by the desire to *acquire* something: a business card, an invite, a job, a connection, a partner or client, or funding for your business. But not only is that approach ineffective, it will also leave you frustrated and exhausted. In fact, a "what's in it for me" mindset is the opposite of what I suggest for developing nourishing business relationships. Instead of throwing business cards at a roomful of people who will likely add them to their recycling bin, I recommend a simple paradigm shift. The best way to become a connector—to build a meaningful and robust network—is to take command and *be the host*. Rather than waiting for an invitation (or to "get" anything at all), *do the inviting yourself.*

Take the next step in the *Gather* phase by channeling your inner Martha Stewart and being the best host you can be. That is the "how can I help" mantra in action. You don't have to wait for permission to immerse yourself in the company you wish to be in. You can arrange and host those gatherings yourself. What you're really asking in this instance is: How can I take a stand in the position of host and decide not only who should attend a gathering, but also why and how?

But it's important to make the distinction between hosting and people pleasing! When you're hosting and making others feel comfortable, you are considering *your* needs just as much as any-one else's. A host doesn't stretch him or herself too thin, or agree to taking on events or actions that they don't have the bandwidth or resources to execute. People pleasing, on the other hand, is moti-vated by what *others* need—and how much they value you—and is often a result of poorly defined boundaries. According to the 2019 *Fast Company* article "How to stop your people-pleasing behavior from limiting your success," people pleasing goes one step beyond graciousness.[1] And it can backfire professionally as "pleasers" are typically seen as less powerful and earn less respect from their col-leagues. While a gracious host—someone who embodies the ethos of the "how can I help" mantra—keeps an eye toward how he or she can make others feel comfortable, a people-pleaser compulsively and continually says "yes" to others' requests, even at the expense of their own mental and physical health. This is an important distinc-tion: I'm not suggesting that you become a pleaser. The "how can I help" method that I espouse is one that elevates you to a more pow-erful position of leadership, connection, and resourcefulness.

A DIFFERENT KIND OF JOMO

Hosting—rather than waiting to be invited—makes connecting easier in two key ways. First, it completely transforms your inner monologue. When you're doing the inviting, any anxiety, fear, or dread you might have about networking can dissolve. Instead of wondering "Will I be invited?" your thoughts can become "Who should I invite?" Asking yourself *that* question immediately puts you into a position of power: *you* are in control. **FOMO** (fear of missing out) can transform into **JOMO**—but not the "joy of missing out" you've probably heard about. In this scenario, JOMO becomes the joy of meeting others. The genius of this strategy is that it elevates you from a position of weakness—wondering what fabulous networking events are transpiring without you—to a position of power and strength. Instead of being a follower, waiting for permission, you become a leader: hosting, connecting, and building relationships, one gathering or call at a time. People will begin to perceive you as a proactive leader: "Did you hear about the gatherings that Susan is hosting?"

The old way of networking is tiring, outdated, and ineffective. It often results in awkward encounters with people we may not find inspiring. When we fall into the networking trap, we can find ourselves making forced connections with people we think are the "right" ones to know. While we wait for an invitation to the networking event or gathering that will put us in proximity to our dream investor, donor, influencer, or mentor—we are in a position of weakness. *Will they want me? Will they invite me?* It's reactive and submissive—not to mention stressful. This waiting approach flips the balance of power out of our favor, and in my experience, it also leads to stagnation and "failure to launch" rather than growth. But you can reclaim your place at the gathering by throwing one yourself. Establishing yourself as someone who organizes and hosts events (even online events)—who gives as well as receives—will also set you up for future invitations and connections.

There's even a term for this in social psychology—*reciprocity*. Reciprocity is the normalized social behavior of responding to a positive action (waving "hello," for example) with another positive action (a wave back).[2] It's the Golden Rule: do unto others as you would have them do unto you. And while it may seem that not everyone follows this rule, most do. When you *do* reach out, connect, and invite, the recipients of your gifts will feel a sense of indebtedness to return that favor to you, but not in a demanding or required way. Whenever you feel like you don't have a "big enough" network, or if you feel you lack meaningful business connections, there's only one person who can fix it: *you*. The good news? There's proof that "inviting to get invited" works. Personally, I can attest to the effectiveness of this method, because I've used it myself for 30 years with great success.

But there is further proof. In 1974, a sociologist at Brigham Young University by the name of Phillip Kunz decided to conduct an experiment on reciprocity.[3] He was curious: What would happen if he sent out holiday cards to complete strangers? Would any of them reply? He compiled a list of 600 random names and accompanying addresses. And as many of us do over the holidays, he mailed out cards to all 600 families on that list. But the difference, of course, was that *he'd never met any of these people*. He included a handwritten note, or a photo of himself with his family, wishing them well during the holiday season. The results were impressive. He got replies: at first, just a few; they trickled in. But soon there was an onslaught—over the course of the holiday season, he received over 200 holiday cards from his list of complete strangers. He was even more surprised by what came back in the mail to him—in some cases, he received lengthy replies. Some people mailed him handwritten letters up to four pages long! And not only that—the correspondences weren't short-lived. He and his family received cards from some of those strangers for 15 years! Kunz's holiday card experiment illustrates the law of reciprocity in action—someone who is initially a stranger can become a long-term, meaningful connection—just because you reached out and gave them a reason to connect with you.

If you're still not convinced, allow me to remind you that you engage in reciprocity every single day, often without realizing it. We all do! It's the reason we say "good morning" back to someone who greeted us in the elevator or smile back at someone we pass on the hiking trail. Sure, there will be a few jerks along the way who break or take advantage of this social norm, but most human beings want to help each other, to connect, and to return kindness. All you have to do is start inviting, and you'll be invited in return. Whatever it is that you're lacking—connections, ideas, invitations to events—start giving them to other people. And soon like the sociologist Kunz, you will see them returned to you. What you also learn from this process is that while you may have once thought, "I really hope this person would invite me to their event," chances are quite good that someone on your invite list felt exactly the same way. Now you have satisfied that person's need to belong. And when someone gives us that gift of *mattering*, even if it's with a simple holiday card, most human beings feel motivated to return that kindness.

DEFINE THE PURPOSE OF YOUR GATHERING

Now that you know it's on you to make invitations yourself—that you reap what you sow in building meaningful connections—it's time to start inviting. But before doing that, there's a key step that many people tend to forget: define the purpose of your gathering, your event, or even your coffee meetup. Many people skip over this important step. But if you haven't set an intention or a goal, what's the point of getting together in the first place? My friend and colleague Morra Aarons-Mele, founder of Women Online and the influencer network The Mission List, suggests that you first take a step back and decide "Why do you want to connect and what are you hoping to get out of it?"

Defining the purpose of your gathering or meeting sounds like common sense, but many fail to take this necessary step. Before you send out any invitations or emails, ask yourself: Are you trying to raise awareness? Are you trying to educate people? Are you trying to fundraise for a cause? Aarons-Mele also suggests being intentional about your time, even if you're not a time-starved CEO running a team of 500 employees. If you can develop discipline around how you spend your time—and who you spend it with—it will serve you for the rest of your life. As you do this, you will find that it requires a healthy dose of "no thank yous"—and that's a good skill to hone as well. (And an antidote to people pleasing!) Even if you're starting out in your career, it pays to be discerning about which events and meetings need to transpire, as well as who and what is worth your time.

As you broaden and build your network, there are different types of people that you will want to connect with: trusted mentors you can get honest advice from, super connectors who can put you in touch with other people, and no-nonsense truth speakers who will give you honest feedback you might need to hear. Before you connect with *anyone*, create a specific goal or intention around each meeting or gathering. Aarons-Mele also told me that she sees young people today, in particular, putting enormous pressure on themselves to build the perfect network or the perfect career. She suggests letting go of that unnecessary weight. She told me, "When I was growing up, we didn't have tech incubators, we just got shitty jobs and figured it out." She likes to tell the young people who come to her for career advice, "just breathe." Neither your career nor your networking building efforts will be a straight linear line—and it's okay. And whether it's your first year in the business world or your fortieth, we can all benefit from returning to the basics. Aarons-Mele suggests, "Think about what's going to make you happy in your work, how much money you need to make—and connection will happen. Your connections come when you do work you love, and you have that spark in you and someone else sees it." Connecting doesn't need to be forced, stressful, or overdone.

HOST RATHER THAN WAIT
TO BE INVITED

Once you start thinking about connecting in this way, it can be incredibly fun. Be the mixologist of your own social cocktail and find ways to bring people together—people you already know or have a way to reach indirectly, and whom you genuinely like or think will get along with each other.

Early in my career at PR Newswire, I spearheaded a monthly gathering for all those I had met working in the communications field. We would meet for breakfast once a month, and every other time we met, each person would bring a new contact to the gathering. This was in 1991, long before the Internet and social media. And those breakfast meetings not only made everyone feel welcome, but they also established me in my career as one of the go-to people for knowledge of the public relations community for recruiting employees, hiring consulting firms, and general information about the industry—not to mention good restaurants and stellar hiking trails.

Today in 2021, you could take these meetings from the comfort of your own home through videoconferencing apps like Zoom. As I write this chapter, the coronavirus pandemic is unfolding across the globe. In a matter of weeks, offices, businesses, schools, and retail establishments have shuttered worldwide in an attempt to slow the spread of the deadly virus. Millions of people across the globe are now working remotely as they are "sheltering in place." It's remarkable and also terrifying at times, to see and feel the entire world changing—with fierce velocity and intensity—as I write these words. The pandemic is sure to have a lasting effect on the way we connect—both online and in person—but the methods I prescribe in this book are impervious to change, pandemic or not. Whether it's online, in real life, or somewhere in between, when you connect with intention and around shared interests, connections will flourish and feed your soul as well as help you reap professional rewards.

So let's say you've decided *why* you're connecting in the first place and *what* you want to get out of it. Now it's time to decide *how* and *with whom* to do it. It doesn't need to be a fancy gathering, and it doesn't need to be a three-hour event. It doesn't have to be a big group of people. It could be a 20-minute call with a few neighbors to brainstorm ways to reduce wildfire risk in your area. And if you're an introvert, *hosting* doesn't have to be a dirty word. Aarons-Mele wisely told me, "Different people have different levels of need for connection." As someone who thrives on human connection—I need that face-to-face time to survive!—this was an important reminder. Everyone is different, in connecting and in life. Some people, like me, thrive on other people and social connections. But others, like Aarons-Mele, don't emotionally need the connections as much—though it can still be a good idea to stay connected.

HOST AN EVENT AROUND
A PARTICULAR ISSUE

Once you've connected with yourself and thought through the intention and purpose of your gathering, another great trick is to plan your gathering around a particular cause or issue. That in itself can align stars that may find themselves creating the magic of a constellation. I've hosted events for people running for office, launching books, as well gatherings to discuss issues such as reproductive rights, climate change, and public health. You could even bring people together over something as simple (or as complex!) as how to handle kids who are constantly staring at their phones. You can literally host events about anything and everything.

Back in the 1990s, for my public relations/communications breakfasts—the intention was about getting people together in the public relations industry. We started with just five people and getting together on a monthly basis. But over time, everybody wanted to be part of this informative and collaborative gathering. One PR person would say to another, "Oh, you've got to meet Susan—she's hosting these monthly gatherings." From there, it exponentially grew. Before long, I was able to secure business from a slew of companies on my prospect list. And not only was this strategy effective from a business perspective, I made friendships with many of those colleagues and clients that have lasted 30 years. Somebody once said to me, "The only difference in deciding which company to give your business to is the specific person you're buying from." It dawned on me: people weren't buying PR Newswire because it was a better service—they were buying because they felt comfortable with the person representing it.

It's worth repeating: people do business with people, and they do business with those they feel aligned with and comfortable. Be somebody that the majority of people want to do business with.

SEEDING RELATIONSHIPS

Once you've established a relationship, it needs tending to or it will die—or at least whither and go dormant for a while. So once you've made that connection, how do you make sure the relationship thrives? Back in the early 1990s when I was managing that sales territory in Southern California, I scheduled time for this activity once per month on a Friday. I would call every single person in my Rolodex and leave a message with their assistant or leave a voicemail. These were the days before email emerged, and even before voicemail was ubiquitous. I'd just leave a quick message to say, "I'm just thinking of you." That was it. There was no ask and no need for a response.

Now that I run a company, it has forced me to be more judicious and thoughtful. At McPherson Strategies, we use a tool called Insightly, which lets me take all my contacts and put them into one database. But back in those early days, I learned everything I know about people skills and how to be responsive from my boss at the time, a woman by the name of Nancy Sells. She was based in Los Angeles—at PR Newswire's regional office. At that time, PR Newswire didn't have an Orange County office. Most people didn't realize PR Newswire had a presence on the West coast, since the company's headquarters was in New York. It was a huge disadvantage because Business Wire, PRN's biggest competitor, was headquartered in San Francisco and had a small team in Orange County. I came from the editorial side of the world and didn't know anything about sales.

But Nancy taught me how to befriend, engage with, and connect people—and that made all the difference. Nancy taught me a critically important skill: Find out what makes people tick. When you meet someone, find out what's interesting to them and what challenges they faced. Then ask yourself: How can I become a resource for that? How can you be the person who knows the best restaurants? How can you be the person to advise where to go on vacation? If you're running a sales territory, your success doesn't solely depend on how well you sell a service or product. The most successful salespeople will be the ones who make themselves a resource and ultimately—a friend who will support them and answer their questions. Nancy and I would spend a day together on sales calls. We were in the car all day long—doing everything *in* the car: eating lunch, putting on makeup, you name it. Back then the cell phones were the size of telephone books, and they were incredibly expensive to use. So instead, we would stop along California's 405 highway and use pay phones to check in on our clients. We'd stand there right off the highway exit, plunking quarters into the pay phone, calling clients to say, "Hey, I'm in the area. I know you're busy, but I'd love to stop by." Back then, we didn't have LinkedIn, email newsletters, CRMs, or smartphones (or even Google Maps). But we were still striving for the same end result that people strive for today. Even though so much has changed with technology and the way we communicate today, we're still cultivating a relationship with a human being who has to make a decisions. Whether or not that person chooses to do business with you ultimately depends on how comfortable they feel with you—how much they trust you. Whether you do it through email, a pay phone call, a telegram, or a text—the goal is the same. You want that person to trust you, to feel that you have a solid relationship. And no matter what the medium, whether it's the tools we use today or the ones that the next generation will use 20 years from now, the intention behind your contact is what matters. Your regular check-ins let that person know: *I see you as a real person; I genuinely care about you and want to connect. Yes, I want to do business with you, but beyond that, I see you as a human being and a friend.*

CREATE A SYSTEM

There are myriad different ways to do these daily check-ins. Aarons-Mele advocates what she calls the "10 touches rule." There are a lot of different versions of this, but in her version, she makes an intentional connection to 10 people in her broader network over email,

LinkedIn, text, or a phone call. She lives in a suburb of Boston, so in her case, a digital connection makes the most sense and she tends to do that rather than a coffee or a meeting. Use whatever method or medium works best for you; just make it a regular habit to seed the meaningful business relationships in your life. If it helps to put some structure around it—such as setting a specific time, like 3 p.m. on Friday—start with that. Soon it will become automatic and seamless, and you will reap untold benefits.

KEEP IT SIMPLE AND START SMALL

Building a network sounds like a daunting task—like running a marathon. But it doesn't have to be overwhelming or draining. Having breakfast with three people sounds pretty easy, right? Let the guests you invite do your legwork for you by inviting a friend. Connections will unfold organically with hardly any effort on your part. All it takes is two committed people to quickly build to four people. Then the next time you meet, ask each of those four to bring a colleague—and voila you already have eight people. And you're well on your way to a network that grows exponentially. And if this method doesn't work for you and you find other tips and tricks that work better—perfect. Because the other big mistake I see people make is becoming married to their "shoulds." Whether it's a conference, mixers, or a meetup—sometimes we feel like we just have to go to them, or we'll miss our chance. Aarons-Mele compares it to dating: when you miss that one event you think, "Oh my God, I missed *the one.*" In this case, meaning the perfect next boss or cofounder that was going to make you rich and famous. She feels that people often put an undue amount of pressure on these types of events, creating a lose–lose situation: if you don't go, you're anxious and upset, and if you *do* go, and you don't meet *the one*, you're still stressed out because it wasn't a good use of your time. To avoid this she offers a tip and suggests looking retrospectively at your calendar: What were the three or four conferences, dinners, or mixers that were really worth the time? Repeat those. Think about the levers that will drive your life forward—and make a point of going *there*. You don't have to exhaust yourself going everywhere and trying every method. Find something that works and stick with it. If you're young and just starting out, you might have a boss who's always telling you to "build a network" and perhaps even offering you tickets to go to this or that event. But it will pay to be as discerning as you possibly can. Because every *yes* you say to one gathering or event is a *no* to something else.

And what if your dream cofounder or client was at the one you said *no* to?

LOCATION, LOCATION, LOCATION

I n a way, an extreme situation that takes the vast majority of global businesses online, like the COVID-19 pandemic, almost forces you to connect in a way you might have previously avoided. Once social distancing was implemented, people found creative ways to connect—they played tennis across rooftops, hopped in their cars to wave homemade birthday posters outside friends' windows, and used Zoom for happy hours, religious celebrations, weddings, and even funerals. Whether you're forced to disrupt your location or not—all of us can benefit from taking a mindset of disrupting our location and using it as an opportunity to connect in a better and perhaps deeper way.

At different points in your life, you will no doubt find yourself conducting business from an entirely new place. Whether you're embarking on a new career in a different industry, moving your company to a new city, or figuring out how to pivot your business during an unprecedented crisis, knowing how to skillfully and artfully build community in a new or different environment will serve you time and time again. When you arrive in that "new" place—whether it's a completely new city, a career change, or adapting to a different way of doing your job—the essential question is the same: How do I build community in a new city, a new field, or a new economy? When you barely know where to get a decent cup of coffee—how do you even begin to think about your connections? The notion of starting from ground zero when you feel like Dorothy landing in Oz can be daunting. I've seen many clients feel paralyzed from a perceived lack of connections in a new city, a new field, or a new space of some kind—instead of seeing it as an opportunity for a reset and a possible pivot. But the reality in these situations is that you have far more resources at your disposal than you might think.

Even if you're not in a "new" location or industry, it's easy to become siloed and feel like you're in a walled-off city of your own. Cate Luzio is the founder of Luminary, a premier collaboration hub for women who are passionate about professional development and expanding their networks. Luzio started Luminary after she realized that women needed a physical—as well as digital—space to meet their learning, development, coworking, and even wellness needs. She points out that even if you're not isolated or in the middle of a significant move, it's easy to become siloed. "It's human nature to get siloed, right?" she says. "So much is digital now, we've forgotten how to connect." Luzio feels that our digital lives have pushed us apart in some ways: we click on LinkedIn or add a friend on Facebook and feel we've "connected," but we haven't. To do that, ask yourself, as Luzio wisely suggests, "How can you be relational versus transactional?" Start by just building a genuine connection with the people around you—no matter their background or experience. Luzio adds, "When you do that, you can learn, inspire, telling stories and bringing in different perspectives, both diversity of thought, and diversity of representation."

VOLUNTEER THROUGH WORK

One way to step out of a transaction mindset—and foster value-based connections, as Luzio suggests—to is to volunteer for organizations that need your help. Getting involved in your local community will let you meet the people there, to find out how you can contribute your skills most meaningfully and to establish a foundation in your new setting. There are myriad ways you can get involved and everything "counts"—nonprofits, political organizations, places of worship, coworking venues, professional training, personal development courses, recreational workshops, classes, local Facebook or LinkedIn groups or Meetups, and PTAs or school boards. By reaching out to the local community in all of these different ways, you will establish new roots. Start with one or two organizations that interest you the most, and in no time, you will forge meaningful relationships, each one building upon the other.

Volunteer service is also an excellent way for companies to engage their employees and help them build new connections and skills, too. Even before the coronavirus pandemic hit in 2020, an unprecedented 4.7 million employees were already working remotely.[1] Many employees were feeling lonely and disconnected. Then COVID-19 hit, and the entire global economy was forced to evolve and operate digitally and remotely as much as possible. In times of crisis, connecting around a common service goal tends to happen organically: everyone in the company comes together to help save the company, to protect each other, or to serve the neediest people in the community. But in times of prosperity, it's still an excellent practice for the company, the community, and the team to join hands around a common service goal. When employees work together in a volunteering capacity, it softens the blow of isolation and provides a dopamine rush from helping and connecting. And often employees can offer skills-based volunteering to organizations in need, which provides countless benefits.

If you are an employee working for a company that doesn't yet serve together—talk to your human resources department or CEO about setting up a program like this. The company can set a certain number of hours for employees to volunteer or set up a skills-based volunteering program where the company can provide paid leave. Larger companies and organizations with more significant resources will have much more leniency around this, of course, but it's fruitful for small businesses, too. Companies may worry they're going to miss their employees' time and energy, but the surprising truth is that employees who volunteer are more productive and satisfied.[2]

As a business owner providing this, you will help your employees feel grounded in the communities from which they operate, which is vitally important to the longevity of your business. Studies have also shown that volunteer work positively affects earnings and wages, and also helps people return to work more rapidly after an interruption—after having children or following an unemployment stint, for example. Research has also shown that volunteering not only creates bonds between colleagues, but also makes employees happier and healthier, and reduces turnover. A 2013 study by the United Health Group found compelling research on how volunteering impacts relationships among employees, and 81 percent said that volunteering with their company or organization strengthened their relationships with their coworkers.[3] The 2016 Deloitte Volunteer Impact Survey found that 92 percent of corporate human resources executives surveyed agreed that contributing business skills and expertise to a nonprofit is an effective way to improve employees' leadership and professional skill sets.[4] Research has also shown that the more connections and touch points a relationship has, the deeper and more meaningful it will be.[5] It makes sense: If you simply sit next to a colleague during the day and your relationship doesn't go any further, it's unlikely to blossom. But if you work together on projects, and share a meal and collaborate on a community project together—serving the people in the surrounding area where you live—you'll develop more touch points, a deeper connection. And you will be happier and more invested in your shared work as a result.

But wait, I don't have time to volunteer—I'm already swamped! You might be surprised to learn what volunteering does to your sense of time. A study in the journal *Psychological Science* found that while it may not be possible to change the number of hours in the day (there are 24 hours, no matter how you slice it), it *is* possible to increase what's known as your time affluence—or your perception of how much time you have.[6] This study found that giving *away* some of your time by spending it on others—like you do when you volunteer, for example—increases one's feeling of time affluence. The reason is that doing things for others gives you a boost of self-efficacy or your feeling of self-worth. And this, in turn, gives you a sense of accomplishment and achievement that begets a feeling of being able to accomplish more in less time. It's as if you simply gain a level of confidence in what you can do with the time that you *do* have, improving your sense of control over getting things done more efficiently.

The takeaway: the next time you feel disengaged at work—or pressed for time—consider volunteering.

JOIN A COWORKING SPACE, EVEN A DIGITAL ONE

If you're launching a business in a new city, joining a local coworking or collaboration community is a great way to integrate yourself into your new zip code—and to boost your productivity and well-being, too. Not only can coworking spaces offer a local perspective, they can also provide community around any interest or affinity group you can imagine. Whether you seek to find other working mothers, people of color, angel investors—or merely a fellow vegan recipe enthusiast—you are sure to find those who share your interests as well as those who will introduce you to experiences you never anticipated. Memberships to coworking spaces have skyrocketed in the last 15 years. In 2020, there were roughly 3.8 million coworking space members globally.[7] All around the world, these virtual communities and physical spaces—like The Cru, The Riveter, Ethel's Club, Luminary, and Conduit House, to name a few—have emerged. These collaborative hubs offer alternatives to people who work independently or remotely to find community, even when traveling or relocating. They have also redefined what an office space means, forever eliminating the notion that a shared workplace should be limited to a particular city or industry. In these spaces, people from different sectors can comingle and cocreate—inspiring each other through conversation at shared tables and through the spaces' events that come with memberships. And as a 2017 *Harvard Business Review* article first noted, coworking spaces aren't really about the spaces themselves anyway, but rather the community.[8] Many studies have proven that telecommuting, without a strong community and support network, leads to an increased feeling of isolation and loneliness, and that the rise of the "gig economy" is one lever driving increased rates of loneliness in today's workers. But coworking spaces and communities can provide an antidote. *Harvard Business Review*'s research showed that 79 percent of members of coworking spaces found that membership expanded their networks. 83 percent said they were less lonely. And a whopping 89 percent said they were happier![9] Research has also found that people who belong to coworking spaces are more likely to report higher levels of "thriving" at work.

Throughout this chapter, we will meet other pioneering coworking space founders. I hope that these origin stories will not only show you how an authentic community is built but also inspire you to seek *your* community—or to create one yourself. In these shared, collaborative workspaces, employees feel connected, supported, and find their work is meaningful. Supporting and funding membership to coworking spaces is another way for companies to invest in their teams, exposing them to a diversity of ideas and information exchange and giving them a community in which they can build social connections and thrive. If they do, they will see a ROI well worth the investment. Whether it's a high-end exclusive club or a free online community, there's a coworking community for everyone. The costs can range anywhere from $45 per month to over $1,000 per month, depending on the space, events, and location. And in the pages that follow, I will share tips for building a similar community if you are strapped for cash. Encouraging that connection—for yourself or for your team—will make everyone feel more supported and in turn, more productive. There's another reason, too: the exposure will bring more people to the fold, increasing awareness about your product or business, which can generate new clients, customers, and revenue. For entrepreneurs and founders, I highly recommend that you encourage your employees to be active in meaningful communities and gathering spaces. Employees and the company will benefit.

Ethel's Club is a social club in New York for people of color. Naj Austin created Ethel's Club, a community that she envisioned through a lens of intentionality and transparency for a physical space where marginalized communities could feel seen. Austin found that there were one-off events like AfroTech or weekend getaways for people of color. But she asked herself, "Why does it always have to be so ephemeral? Why can't we have something that's constant and consistent that centers on who we are?" So in January 2019 she simply wrote her idea down in the notes app on her smartphone. A month later, she created an Instagram account for Ethel's Club, and it started securing a ton of interest and traction—people were tagging their friends and saying, "This looks awesome." Soon the *New York Times* wrote about it and then it really took off. Ethel's Club offers free mental health services three days a month for anyone to book time with a therapist inside the club. They offer events that are open to the public, it's not for members only, and they created many online events when the pandemic hit.

When I asked Austin what could be done about making amenities like coworking spaces more available for marginalized communities, she responded:

> *Companies* need to be the ones to make their communities available for people. It's time to take the onus off of the individual and put it back on the company—make your community available for all people. Marginalized communities have never had access to country clubs or these sort of private spaces. When I started Ethel's Club, they didn't even know what a social club was. We had a lot of people say, "This sounds awesome, but what is it?" So companies need to do their part in making these types of things available for all.

I encourage you—whether you are merely joining a physical or digital community or starting one yourself—to ask yourself: Is this community inclusive? Has enough been done to make it available for every race, sex, creed, religion, and especially for the marginalized, disenfranchised, and underrepresented? If not, ask yourself what you can do to change that. And if you can't do that—ask yourself why you're joining and whether or not that step is the right one for the greater good.

Amy Nelson is the founder of The Riveter, a national membership network of community, content, resources, and coworking spaces built by women but open to all. For Nelson, it was a physical transformation of a different sort that inspired her to create The Riveter: pregnancy. Nelson was working as a litigator at a law firm when she was pregnant with her first child, and as a seeker of community, she thought it would be a good idea to talk to working moms at her firm. She imagined discussing how they navigated pregnancy, the transition back from leave, and tips for continuing your career afterward. Nelson said, "I looked up and realized—wait, there are no working moms in my litigation group—why have I never noticed that?" It wasn't something she'd been focused on. She adds, "There were 17 apps that could tell me my baby was the size of a strawberry, but there was nothing to help me through the process of telling my boss I was pregnant or to coach me on how to navigate this period of life."

And so she created The Riveter—a community that acknowledges that women *do* take their careers very seriously, and they want to talk about and connect around it. But as she points out, "The baseline conversation in our culture about working women is still stuck on the same question, 'Can women have it all?' and no one has bothered to ask the next 17 questions." But through her work at The Riveter, that's exactly what she pioneers: facilitating those next steps in the conversation—acknowledging that females are the majority in the workforce, they're figuring it out, and they need community and connection around it.

Tiffany Dufu is another pioneering community founder who looked around and couldn't find the community she wanted, so she created it. It dawned on her that most companies and organizations care about their employees only as it relates to business. But she wanted a community that is agnostic to business, one that acknowledges all of the different aspects of our humanity. To meet that need, she founded The Cru, a peer coaching platform for women looking to accelerate their professional and personal growth. When you join The Cru, you're asked to develop your intentions, goals you want to achieve over the next 12 months that can relate to any aspect of your life. It could be a promotion, getting 500 more Instagram followers, or losing 10 pounds. Dufu recognized that especially for women, the ability to feel happy, healthy, and whole—and to thrive at work professionally—is very much connected to what happens in other aspects and parts of one's life. The Cru leverages technology to do that, to help facilitate that human connection.

Here's how it works: you apply to the Cru, and the algorithm matches you with nine other women in your city based on your values, personality, demographics, and goals. It's not complicated technology—not any more sophisticated than what eHarmony uses to match couples—but the idea is that it's much more robust than forcing people to show up at a cocktail party or a dinner party, awkwardly introduce themselves to strangers, and then exchange business cards. The Cru is also unique because it is biased toward diversity. Dufu says,

> I believe that you can achieve incredible outcomes in your life simply by bouncing ideas off of and collaborating with people who are very different from you, but unfortunately we live in a world where most of us are communicating with people in the same echo chamber or ecosystem.

Dufu explains that human beings are wired to gravitate toward similar people, so even if you work in a diverse workplace, you're still not very differentiated, as you come from the same industry or same set of knowledge about something together. So what she set out to create with The Cru is a way to *intentionally* match women who come from different industries, have different family configurations, or come from different racial, ethnic backgrounds. The majority of women in The Cru are women of color, because if you tell an algorithm, "I want ten women and I want them to be diverse," you're always going to end up with majority women of color in a Cru. The Cru also has a fascinating way of helping its members solve problems, by asking a set of questions akin to the Socratic method, or the way a therapist might help you see hidden strengths or perceive things from a different angle.

Dufu says, "You can hear Cru members asking one another these questions at our events." They are questions like, "What have you tried so far?" "What would happen if you asked for exactly what you wanted?" "What do you feel like is the biggest strength that you are bringing to the situation?" or "Who do you feel like are the people who need to be engaged here to solve this issue?" Dufu points out that these questions illustrate the power of having a Cru or any collaborative community in which you can break the cycle of going around in circles or getting stuck on a particular problem.

"Sometimes we get in a rumination loop," she says, "but you want to try to drive your Cru member toward action." Action—that's the key.

Whether you join a coworking space like Ethel's Club, The Riveter, The Wing, Luminary, The Cru, or Soho House—or one of the many others across the globe—or not, the ethos of these inspiring hubs can guide you. Connect with others on who will inspire you to take action, to make tangible progress toward your goal. Whether you choose to join one of these spaces or to build community organically yourself—coffee by coffee, Zoom call by Zoom call—your cohort is out there waiting for you to connect.

JOIN AN ONLINE COMMUNITY, GROUP, OR MEETUP

While some coworking spaces and communities are on the expensive side, there are plenty of online groups and meetups that are entirely free. The League of Badass Women, Tuenighters, The Woolfer, and Women Who Whiskey are four vibrant examples. Another such group is *The What*—a weekly newsletter with exceptional recommendations and a highly engaged community of women and *Perennial* readers from around the globe, founded by serial entrepreneurs Gina Pell and Amy Parker. Pell and Parker accomplished an astonishing feat in building The What: they managed to create an online community of 35,000 women without trolls, negative comments, or disparagement. The attention and skill with which they built The What is a shining illustration of how to build *any* community of human beings—whether it's for a gathering at your dinner table, a client event, or a community baseball game. Pell says that whether you're trying to build community or write marketing copy, or establish any relationship with another human being, the way you do that is by talking to people the way you would speak to a friend. It was this talking to their community—from a place of curiosity, warmth, discovery, and relatability—that allowed them to create a thriving, highly engaged, and incredibly supportive online community. Pell says that she and Parker got into this business because they wanted to connect, inform, and engage women. It started so small with just a hundred of their personal friends and a few avid readers, and now it's grown to over 35,000 women. But the friendliness, kindness, and support that you see in that group is a reflection of the relationship that Pell and Parker have with each other.

Pell says, "We've been friends for 20 years. We absolutely have each other's back. We absolutely trust each other. We have a lot of fun together." And she says that the civility, kindness, gentleness, support, and enthusiasm that emerge from that group comes largely comes from the way Pell and Parker treat each other. The community is incredibly diverse: there are members who are famous household names as well as those who live an entirely different life, like a single mother from a small logging town near Ukiah.

To build new connections when you've moved or are just starting out, Pell recommends finding a group—even a free one—that engages whatever kind of mindset you want to attract. For Pell and Parker, it was what they call a "perennial mindset"—a phrase that Pell coined. A perennial is a woman who's interested in growing, learning, exploring, collaborating, working on the hard stuff, and finding other people who want to do that. She adds, "You're not going to vibe with everybody, and that's fine. It's a numbers game—proactively grow your network organically person by person, until you find people who can help you solve your problem." If you keep looking, you will find a team of people who are going to help propel you forward. "But nothing's going to happen if you're sitting in your house," Pell said. "You absolutely can't do it on your own."

Gina Bianchini is another serial entrepreneur who has been tackling the question of how people best connect through online communities for the last decade. Bianchini is the founder of Ning, which allowed people to create their own personal social networks, and Mightybell, a collaborative app that inspired people to accomplish things in small steps. Now Bianchini is founder and CEO of Mighty Networks, which offers companies comprehensive connecting tools (such as online courses or a membership site) for their brand. Using Mighty Networks, companies can essentially create and charge for the ability to run courses, to have mastermind groups, and to have a community—and they can charge for any or all pieces of that. The beauty of this system is that it's all under their brand, instantly available, on every platform, with all of these pieces in one place. Why have your community on Facebook, your courses on Coursera, or use other platforms that you don't own?

Bianchini tells me that when your brand or small business has people coming to all of these different platforms for disparate features of your business (such as courses or community, for instance), the connection gets lost. When you're on Facebook, your connection is to Facebook and no longer to St. Helena Yoga, or whatever the business might be. And one of the great things about having everyone all under one platform—one mighty network, as it were—is that you can get feedback from them and innovate on that feedback much faster. Bianchini explained this to me by sharing the insights she gleaned over developing the online course element of her business:

> In late 2015, early 2016 we started hearing from a lot of our early customers, "Why don't you guys just build online courses?" This platform is great, they said, but I would really love to have my online courses here. It kept coming up over and over again, so we built online courses into the platform. But when I was talking to other businesspeople who'd built online courses previously, they always prefaced it by saying, "Well, I have 10 years of online course experience, and I've been building and running an online course for a zillion years . . ." So I literally thought that you had to have a master's degree in running an online course. I thought I had no business running an online course—but then I realized that I didn't have to build the entire thing all at once. I could start small and iterate. So I started with what I called a mastermind group and offered it to our paying customers. Over 500 people signed up and we quickly got great feedback on what worked and what was missing. We have a really good sense, at any given time, what are the resources people need? The feedback is so much faster, which allows us to get better faster.

DON'T DISCOUNT THE POWER
OF RANDOM CONNECTIONS

Sometimes the best connections are made with great intentions, and other times they are accidental or unexpected. As you build a community in a new city, in a new industry, or in whatever form of disruption you may face—don't discount the seemingly fleeting or random connections you make along the way. Many of the most fruitful and powerful relationships I've had in my professional life have come from my involvement in a virtual or online group. What you invest in these seemingly "random" connections, you will reap. Keep those connections in your mind as you move through the different phases of your career, and stay open to the possibilities that can come long term.

As an example of this, Aarons-Mele says her entire business was built on a random connection. She met the founder of BlogHer, Lisa Stone, while she was in Mexico on a work getaway trip. Stone and Aarons-Mele started talking, and Stone revealed that she was starting a new company called BlogHer. At the time, Aarons-Mele was a political consultant. "Lisa asked me to start writing for BlogHer, and then I just got thrust into this world of women in community online—and about five years later, I started my business, Women Online." Today Aarons-Mele still works with a lot of the original people from her BlogHer days—women who were very early bloggers, and those women are still very much in her life.

Aarons-Mele's experience is not unusual. In 1973, the sociologist Mark Granovetter found that when a random sample of professionals found a new job, 82 percent of them found it through a contact that they saw only occasionally or rarely.[10] Although in many cases you will forge a deep, meaningful friendship, a contact doesn't have to become a best friend forever, or even someone you see on a regular basis, for you to provide meaningful and powerful contributions to each other's lives. Those looser ties in your life are quite important, especially when you view them as much. Whether your ties are weak or strong, once in a decade, or coffee every Tuesday, they are all critical to the social fabric of your life. These looser or more random connections can, of course, deepen. But even if they don't, they still hold immense value. The LinkedIn contacts you barely know, the neighbors you wave at but would hardly call close friends, the person you met at a conference and barely recall— these are what social psychologists call "bridging capital." These are the diverse range of voices and ideas that expose you to new ideas, opportunities, experiences, and quite possibly—careers, too. Studies show that people who have a broader and more wide-ranging network of these weaker ties are more likely to be successful.[11] And research has also shown that people with these types of networks are more open-minded, feel a stronger sense of connection to their community, and are more likely to be able to mobilize support for a cause.[12]

Cate Luzio of Luminary points out that the reciprocation on either side of the relationship doesn't have to come immediately. In any connection, there's reciprocity, but sometimes people—women in particular—don't think about it in this way. She says that instead, they tend to think of it like, "Oh, I have to say yes because I don't want to be impolite, or I want something out of that connection, and I haven't actually reciprocated." But reciprocity can come in a month, or it can come seven years later. You also need, even with a newer connection or someone you've just met in a business setting, to be open and honest about what you are trying to accomplish. Luzio says, "People don't have ESP about what you're trying to achieve—unless you've put it out there in the world, people don't know." She recommends that if you want to be on a board, tell people, or they won't know. If you need to sell more bracelets, or you want to be a coach, or get more clients with a banker, whatever it is: put it out there.

"Business won't just come to you because you're a nice person. You've got to be out there looking for it, and part of that is making real connections to develop that business."

EMBRACE THE S-CURVE

Building a network of friends and colleagues, like any endeavor, is a process. Even if you're doing everything I've prescribed: joining local meetups, volunteering, reaching out to the people you know, staying open to the possibilities of new connections—starting fresh in any location can feel like a slog. If you've experienced this, don't get discouraged, Eventually, your efforts will pay off. There's even a visual—as well as mathematical—model that illustrates this process of growth, whether it's growing your network, a new business, or any new skill.

The S-curve is a concept that was initially popularized by Ian Rogers in 1962.[13] It was meant to help us understand how quickly an innovation would be adopted or diffused. But Whitney Johnson, CEO of WLJ Advisors and one of the 50 leading business thinkers in the world, recognized it as a way to help us understand how we learn and grow. Whitney is also the author of several bestselling books, including *Disrupt Yourself*, which covers this concept. The S-curve is a brilliant visual model for building a network, especially if you're starting over in a new location or field. It can even be a good model for what developing a relationship looks like. As Johnson describes, if you think about the shape of the S-curve—the low end appears to be slow because the exponential growth is not yet noticeable. Then when you get to the steep part of the S you are in hyper-growth, and at the high end, you reach saturation—the growth tapers off. Whenever you start something—moving to a new city, writing a book, start a new job—you're at the launch point of that S-curve. Growth is there, but it looks like it's really slow. Johnson describes it as that lily pad of learning: the lily pads aren't yet apparent, and it's a slog. But then you move into the steep part of the curve, and you're in hyper-growth. That's where things are hard, but they're not too hard, and some elements are easy, but not too easy. It's super exhilarating. And when you learn how to connect with people really well, you are on the sweet spot of that curve. But anytime you're starting fresh in some way, you're going to be entering the slow, slog-like phase of that curve, where it can feel like you don't know anyone or your efforts to connect aren't really bearing any fruit—but they will.

GET UNCOMFORTABLE, BE BRAVE

Though some people like myself are natural connectors, none of us are immune from fear. Though it *is* an art, connecting is not without fear and discomfort. Like anything worth doing, connecting requires being brave. Amy Nelson prescribes "getting comfortable with being uncomfortable." Professional relationship building is also a skill, and just like any skill in business—from learning Excel shortcuts to building revenue models to making a pitch to a potential client—what you practice becomes more comfortable. Nelson suggests using volunteer experiences to practice building professional relationships. Volunteer experience is a perfect opportunity to take risks like cold outreach to people, especially when it is a cause that you care about. Nelson says that she learned many of her networking and community-building skills through her roles as a volunteer. She knocked on doors for political candidates, which gave her practice hearing a "no" and learning that even if you hear no 99 percent of the time, it doesn't eliminate the power of that one yes that you may ultimately get. All you need is *one* yes. Nelson says,

> I got turned down, and I learned to operate in rooms with people I didn't know and later, all of that practice with rejection made raising venture capital money so much easier, because I knew that most times you would hear, "No," but somebody will say, "Yes."

Nelson also suggests that if there is someplace you desperately want to be—a company you desperately want to work for—go talk to someone within the HR department. If you really want to work for Nestle, for example, try to meet someone who works in HR at Nestle and say, "What do I need to do so that I can work here in three to five years?" Don't be afraid to be very direct, ask for connections, and reach out to the people who can give you candid answers. Remind yourself often of Nelson's advice: "We have to do things that scare us." When I asked her where she got the courage to be brave, she said that when she got to law school at NYU, there was a doubtful voice in her head. It said: *Whoa, I do not belong in this room.* She called her father and told him that, and he said, "You belong in any room you want to be in."

"The truth is," she added, "any one of us belongs *anywhere* we want to be—but to be there, we have to make the choice to step into that room." Nelson says that *you* are the only person who can do it—no one's going to do it for you—so be brave enough to step into the room. She also added that though we fear it, it's very unlikely that someone's going to say to you, "You don't belong here." *You're* the one who's holding yourself back, but the more you network and work in the community of people living the life or building the career that you would like to have, the more likely you are to do it.

Nothing worth doing is easy, even building a constellation. It always takes that first step, finding that first link to another star—but the payoff, when it works, is huge.

ZOOM CALLS, DMS, IRL MEETINGS, AND SNAIL MAIL, OH MY!

OK, so let's say you're getting the hang of the *Gather* concept, and you're getting more confident about making new connections. Armed with the tool of asking "how can I help?" you feel more comfortable, too. But there's always the question of the *how* and the *where* once you know that a meeting will transpire. Business meetings used to take place primarily in one of two scenarios: over a meal (coffee, lunch, drinks) or in a conference room. But now? Deciding where to execute your gathering can cause decision fatigue even for the most skilled executive. Should you gather on Zoom or Microsoft Teams? Or is Google Hangouts better? What about a pop-up event? Would a dinner party work best? No one can deny the magic that comes from meeting in real life (IRL). You can learn so much about a person from their body language, how—and when—they arrive, their tone of voice, as well as how they treat other people around you, particularly greeters, waiters, or baristas. But not every meeting needs to happen face-to-face.

Science reveals that in some instances, yes—an in-person conversation can't be beat. But in March 2020—when COVID-19 forced all business meetings abruptly online—it begged the question: Which meetings really *are* necessary to have in person, and which can be just as effective online? I'd argue that an online gathering can be more surprisingly powerful, when used effectively.

MAXIMIZE EACH TYPE OF MEETING (IN PERSON VERSUS DIGITAL)

I've always run my consulting firm, McPherson Strategies, remotely. I've long understood that online meetings and digital spaces are hugely valuable for the growth of any business. Far more than the venue, what matters most is genuine connection. In 2019, I racked up hundreds of thousands of miles in airline travel—zipping from New York to Shanghai, to San Francisco, and beyond to connect with clients, partners, and colleagues. Of course, that all came to a screeching halt. When the coronavirus pandemic hit—and meeting IRL disappeared practically overnight—the entire world began to see video and digital communication differently. Forced by a global lockdown and physical separation, people began using digital communication tools as they were originally intended: to connect as human beings. A coworker or colleague's humanity was no longer covered by their polished work attire or crisply delivered speech. Yelping dogs screeched in the background of All Hands meetings; five-year-olds burst into view during job interviews. The line between work and home became ever blurrier, as working from home (WFH) became the default across the globe. Connecting digitally was no longer relegated to the next best option; it was the *only* option. While the world was starved for face-to-face connection, and it was clear that in many cases that was still the better option, it was also apparent that as businesspeople, there was more juice to squeeze out of our virtual meetings and events. The initial environmental impact of global WFH was also clear: the smog hovering above Los Angeles dissipated, the canals in Venice cleared. As the world paused and waited to go back to our commutes and offices, many wondered: Which meetings really *should* happen online—even once the pandemic is behind us?

When deciding whether to meet in person or online, consider the goal of the meeting. Do you need to build trust? Make an ask? Make an introduction? Zoom meetings are efficient and can be geographically diverse. A two-second retweet can go a long way—and doesn't require you to get dressed up, leave home, and go to an event. Connecting in this way allows you to build relationships over time with small gestures—video chats, Instagram comments, congratulatory notes, and sharing articles. These and other digital "deposits" into a relationship "account" can accumulate into a significant investment over time. But while you *can* build trust digitally—especially using Zoom and other video platforms—meeting virtually isn't quite as satisfying or productive. Group discussions over video, for instance, are especially challenging since facial cues and expressions become harder to read, technical glitches sometimes arise, let alone those awkward interruptions.

In-person gatherings are by far the most real, intimate, and meaningful. I would never recommend that anything replace the pure joy and magic of real connection and trust that takes place when individuals gather together. Science backs this up: in many cases, face-to-face meetings are ideal because they build trust in a way that digital communication cannot. In 2015, *Fast Company* shared research from researchers at the University of Chicago and Harvard in an article called "The Science of When You Need In-Person Communication."[1] The researchers illuminated the significance of the small ways that people touch in face-to-face meetings to build trust—shaking hands, opening a door for each other, ceremoniously exchanging business cards, or giving a business-like pat on the arm at the end of a meeting. While these small acts of touch might seem insignificant, they are quite powerful signals of warmth and a shared sense of connection. You may not consciously think, "hey, I trust this person," when someone pats you on the arm. But an unspoken connection is established. Your brain reacts in a positive way. When you shake hands with someone, that human touch lights up the reward center in your brain, causing you to feel a surge of good feelings.[2] Researchers have also found that when negotiators shake hands with each other, they are more honest and open, and reach better outcomes.[3] The takeaway: meeting in person makes it more likely that you will come to a cooperative agreement or build trust. Consider, too, the message it sends to a client when you fly across the country—or even just across town—to appear in person for a meeting or event. That sacrifice of valuable time and effort sends a powerful message: this relationship is important.

Whether you're on a Zoom line, sitting in a conference room, going on a walk-and-talk, or clinking wine glasses in a restaurant—acknowledge everyone in the room, especially those hired to support the event, who are often overlooked. Every single person deserves attention, kindness, consideration, and compassion. In-person meetings can also give you opportunities to meet other people in the host's organization or to show off your favorite local haunts for out-of-town visitors. From an interpersonal vantage point, I find in-person meetings lead to more fluid conversations, which can be helpful in some instances. If you need to build trust or want honesty, focus, and connection—a deepening a bond—then meeting in person is by far the best.

Some people don't realize how easy it is to strike up a genuine kinship with someone online. I have met many people over the years online who later became close friends. We started by striking up a wonderful correspondence, and in some cases, it wasn't until three years later that I met them in person. Katie Rosman is a reporter for the *New York Times* whom I was connected with on social media. Afterward, we began staying in touch by writing each other notes and emails. When we finally met in person in 2019, we instantly felt much more deeply in sync than a "social media connection." We'd been communicating on a human level: we both lost our mothers and had already bonded over that shared grief; we understood each other. Even though we first connected in a professional capacity, we didn't let that stop us from sharing our humanity—a shared pain. I'm certainly not advocating that you go tweeting about your personal problems to your clients and coworkers. But I fervently believe that closeness, vulnerability and business *can* intersect. Words are powerful. Digital missives can shrink physical separation, build rapport, and pave the way for a deeper relationship to emerge in person later.

HOW TO MAKE ZOOM (AND OTHER MEETING PLATFORMS) MORE PERSONAL

Fran Hauser is a startup investor and advisor, funding and advising consumer-focused companies such as HelloGiggles, Levo, Mogul, The Wing, and Gem & Bolt. Formerly digital president for Time Inc.'s Style and Entertainment Group, she is also a philanthropist and advocate for women in business. Hauser says that in virtual meetings, to make them a bit more personal and connected, she recommends starting the meeting by following up on something someone said in the last call. One example of how to do this is to follow up on something that was discussed in the prior week's call: "How did that client pitch go, Susan?" Or if it's not a recurring meeting, see if you can find something else to ask about right off the bat. Was there a local event that transpired where that person lives that you could ask about? Hauser points out that all of us— no matter what position we're in, no matter what the nature of the business relationship—need to feel seen and psychologically safe. Hauser shared with me that she feels this is extremely important. In fact, in 2016 Google conducted research to find out what created the best "teams." They wanted to find out: What makes teams productive? It was believed that they might find the best teams were those with the brightest members or the people who are agile thinkers in intense situations. But that's not at all what they found. Instead, what Google's research on teams turned up was that the most effective teams were the ones that created the most psychological safety.[4] When team members felt seen and heard, they performed better. And since digital or virtual meetings like those on Zoom and Hangouts can feel more distant and less personal, Hauser's tip is a good one: circle back and let them know you were listening. In some way, let them feel seen and heard.

OTHER WAYS TO CULTIVATE CLOSENESS DIGITALLY

Michael Ronen, a creative director interested in the design of transformative, immersive experiences, wanted to explore how to create digital intimacy in the time of physical distancing. Alongside the Co-Reality Collective, an organization that describes itself as "an autonomous distributed collective devoted to the invention of the next phase of what is real," Ronen developed a virtual party to see if it was possible to cultivate closeness and deep connection while together virtually. The party was called Bodyssey—"a party inside the human body."[5] There were different activities in each of the unique "rooms" or parts of the body, tied to the theme of that particular body part. For instance, there was concert listening in the "ear," cerebral conversation in the "brain," and spiritual experiences in the "third eye." What Ronen and his cocreators learned is that first, digital intimacy is possible. Ronen defines digital intimacy as "the feeling of looking into someone's soul, even if they are in a different continent." What he learned is that for true intimacy to happen online, especially via virtual meeting technology, a group of about six people feels like the right number. While there were certainly experiences in The Bodyssey that were much larger—like concerts and dance parties—for the more vulnerable sharing and connecting, six felt like the right size.

Ronen also found that there were many ways to foster digital intimacy. When you can share the same physical space, there are other spaces that you *can* share: the same physical state (like moving to the same beat, or getting in water—yep, a bathtub!), a similar space (like looking outside at the moon), tasting the same food or drink, or using the same or similar set of props of costumes. In some instances, such as The Bodyssey, using the physical space around you in your home, rather than blocking it out like you typically do on a Zoom call, can foster connections. If you're hosting the video call, you could ask each of your team members to meet in the "conference room," creating the sense that you are together. You could use the same Zoom background, for instance. Or you could simply get creative with where that "conference room" is in your space at home and it could create some connection, comradery (and perhaps a bit of humor) when sharing how you came to select the location you chose.

Of course, I'm not suggesting that you hold your next team online meeting while submerged in your bathtub, but creative uses of these platforms like The Bodyssey reveal how much room for innovation there is when we connect digitally. When we create online gatherings thoughtfully, there's still much room for intimacy and deep connection.

MAKE THE MOST OUT OF EACH MEETING

There are only 24 hours in a day no matter how you slice it. Yet most of us feel our time is increasingly scarce. Especially when you own a business, making the most of meeting times is a high priority. Whether you've decided to take the meeting in an online hashtag conversation or over coffee: prepare ahead of time. Take proactive steps to keep the conversation focused and appropriately brief. Remind yourself of your goal: Do you want to get a job interview? Do you desire a speaking opportunity? Do you want to get your new product reviewed by media? At the end of this particular meeting—what does success look like? Force yourself to answer that question. (If you don't know the answer, ask yourself why you set it up in the first place!) Before the meeting, do some scenario planning: What if it doesn't go well? What if the conversation veers off course? What could you do to steer it back into a productive direction? Of course, you can't walk into a meeting with a robotic, prescriptive mindset and expect to have a fruitful relationship transpire. Look at these initial meetings as a learning opportunity and focus on the other person: What can I learn from them? As my late father always said:

brevity is the key. You want to leave them wanting more. If your meeting, pitch, or presentation is slated for 45 minutes, deliver 30 minutes of material and then offer 15 minutes for a Q&A discussion. Don't just spray information at the audience; they will want to participate, to interact, and to engage. Always offer that—whether it's in a meeting or in a presentation. People sell themselves short when they have a big meeting with an important client and think, "I only have one shot."

But life doesn't work that way, right? If your internal voice during that conversation is saying, "I have to perform and impress this person," you won't be yourself. You'll be a nervous, anxious persona of the real you. But when you decide to cultivate a long-term relationship, you don't have to get everything accomplished in 45 minutes. You've got a lifetime to collaborate, to solve problems, to get to know each other better—and to make things happen.

JOIN EVENTS AND GATHERINGS THAT ARE LEARNING HUBS

Whether it's virtual or in person, never miss an opportunity to attend an event or meeting where you can learn from others. This is what Alison Gelles, the executive director of Renaissance Weekend, calls a "listening tour." "I love going on listening tours," she says, "to learn more about people, see what they're about, what they need, and how I can help." A listening tour is simply taking the opportunity to attend an event—whether it's a conference, a meeting, or a call—where it's your singular focus to listen and to learn from others. In fact, this is one of the key tenets of the Renaissance Weekend events that Gelles oversees. Renaissance Weekend was founded in 1981 by Linda and Philip Lader, the former US ambassador to the Court of St. James's, to foster the candid exchange of ideas among innovative leaders from diverse fields. It was created to build relationships, make connections, break down hierarchy, and help people broaden their perspective beyond their day-to-day responsibilities, and to help bridge the professional, age, racial, religious, political, and other divides of contemporary American society. Essentially, it forces people to escape their bubbles and echo chambers, and to consider global issues from a 10,000-foot view or from a different perspective. "That in itself," Gelles said, "is a lost art." What's brilliant about Renaissance Weekends is their intergenerational, interdisciplinary diversity of attendees, including politicians, educators, elementary schoolteachers, kindergarten teachers, nurses, caretakers. Many have young children in tow, and they, too, from the tween to the six-year-old are invited to participate. The entire weekend is orchestrated around forging unexpected bonds and learning.

Over the course of the weekend, you might find an astrophysicist talking about emerging research, a CEO revealing astute learnings on romantic love, and a professor discussing how to cope with a loved one's tragic suicide. No topic is off limits—and everyone is stripped of their ego, their status, and their title. The connection that transpires from that place of equal footing is quite magical. Every single person is on a first-name basis, from the high-powered business executive to the eight-year-old, stripped down in a way that encourages connection without transactional elements. As Gelles describes it, "People are coming together to give attention to other people's interests, aspirations, and hobbies—to foster an extended family."

When I distill the essence of my philosophy—the lost art of connecting—I often share tales from Renaissance Weekends as a perfect illustration. It's the perfect example of how a constellation comes together. A kindergarten teacher listening to the social activist shares these insights with a Bitcoin expert who just received advice from an astronaut—this is what nontransactional networking looks like. Each of these humans is engaging in a dialogue together with one shared and simple goal: to listen. I urge you to take that ethos into each meeting, interaction, and connection you make.

When you genuinely view people as a gateway to deeper learning, your perception will be different. What might have previously been seen as dollar signs—or a tally against your sales quota—becomes something much greater: vignettes and jumping- off points for collaboration on a grand scale. If you can resist the urge to concern yourself with appearance and just listen with an open mind, magic can transpire—and that person's "status," as well as your own, can melt away. Even if you don't attend a specific event like Renaissance Weekend—you can adopt its mindset to transform the way you conduct your business outreach.

LISTEN. (NO, REALLY)

Perhaps even more important than keeping the meeting or conversation brief—wherever it transpires, even if it's in an elevator—is to listen intensely while you are there. It sounds obvious to the point of absurdity. But human beings are *notoriously bad* at listening. Not only do we stink at it—we're not interested in it either! Dr. Julian Treasure is a sound and communication expert whose mission is to help people and organizations listen better and create healthier and more effective sound, including speaking. His five TED Talks have been watched more than 100 million times. His TED Talk "How to speak so that people want to listen" is in the top 10 TED Talks of all time. But his TED Talk on *how to listen* received only about 10 percent as many views. (Ah ha! We want people to listen *to us*—but we're not so interested in listening *to them*.) We may not want to listen, but it's a crucial key to forming genuine connections! Whether you're discussing a new venture face-to-face or advocating for an issue online—your aptitude for listening will greatly impact your ability to connect. If you can improve your listening skills, you will stand out—people want to be heard, and they will notice.

A key distinction that most people overlook: listening and hearing are not the same thing. Hearing is connected to the old reptilian—*Is that a tiger I hear?*—part of the brain. Hearing works faster than vision and is a very different thing than listening. Listening is the mental process of selecting things to pay attention to and then ascribing meaning to them. It's a skill. Ever heard of selective listening? Like when you ask someone to take out the trash but they claim, "I didn't hear you!" In truth, all listening is selective: we each retain sounds differently. We can walk out of the same conference with 500 other people with a diverging interpretation of what was shared. Each individual's listening is unique—as unique as their fingerprints. Human beings listen through a set of filters, meaning that we ascribe different meaning to what we hear. Considering, this is a great way to communicate more effectively. If you consider how people listen, whether your audience is one person or a thousand, then you can hit the bulls-eye instead of missing the target altogether. Again it's about tuning into your audience and this notion of receiving information.

Dr. Treasure recommends a process called RASA for skilled communication: receive, appreciate, summarize, ask. When you *receive*, you're looking at the person who's speaking, paying attention to them with every part of your body. Face them and actually *take in* what they're saying—show them that you're doing that by not typing, talking, texting, or tweeting. Remind yourself that your only job in that moment is to *absorb* what they have to say. Whether in person or online—sit in the receiving seat first.

The appreciate step includes nodding along, making sounds, gestures, or movements of affirmation and engagement. The summarize step is what Dr. Treasure calls "closing doors in the corridor of your conversation." That's when you confirm that you're on the same page: "So we've agreed this," or, "So I understand X. Is that right?" Then you can shut that door on that part of the conversation and move on. You've agreed or confirmed that you have both walked away with the same understanding of what was communicated. Next, *ask questions* like why, what, how, who, when, which, where, or tell me more. When someone feels as though they don't get heard or they can't get into a conversation, Dr. Treasure suggests that they ask questions of the other person. That's showing engagement. Questions like, "Oh really? Tell me more." Or "Can you say more about that?" Or "That's interesting." The other person gets energized, and so will you. It's another tip that sounds too obvious to mention. But it's like choosing the salad over the fries. We know we *should*—but we don't always do it.

One likely culprit of our failure to listen well? Our insatiable drive for distraction. Treasure champions a quote by the American psychiatrist Scott Peck, "You cannot truly listen to another human being and do anything else at the same time." But how many times has someone said to you, "Yeah, I'm listening" but they are swiping on their phone, eating a sandwich, or follow your question with, "Wait, I just have to send one email." According to Dr. Treasure, "Listening requires 100 percent of your attention." But unfortunately, what most people do, is faux or partial listening. Think about a time in a recent business conversation or meeting where you were half listening. What might you have missed—a key insight or vitally important fact? An important lead? Knowledge that might prevent future mistakes?

Next time: receive rather than react.

Another tip for better listening in meetings? Dr. Treasure says speaking and listening are not in a linear (first this, then that) relationship. It's not: I speak, you listen. Instead, listening and speaking bounce off of each other in a circular and dynamic way. The way I speak *affects* the way you listen. The way you listen affects the way I speak—which then affects the way you speak. Improving your listening capabilities is one of the best ways to forge deeper connections. It's a skill you can improve and use to amplify the depth of your relationships, simply by being more intentional, by choosing to take in information.

"Listening is the doorway to understanding," Dr. Treasure says, "it's very difficult to inspire people if you're not speaking appropriately to them." One simple way to improve your listening prowess is to practice sitting in silence. When you're still and quiet, you begin to hear sounds that were there all along, but you were too distracted to notice. Of course, listening on Zoom or another digital platform is even more challenging than doing so IRL. In a virtual meeting, you're usually staring at your own face in addition to those of your colleagues or clients. (*Is that spinach in my teeth?*) You're also not as accountable: a quick text, a subtle email check—myriad escapes from a less-than-riveting presentation are within reach. Add to that the likelihood that a partner, child, or roommate is also WFH—intent listening may well be a pipe dream! Hold yourself accountable or at least make it harder to get pulled away: shut the door, leave your cell phone in another room, put the dog in a crate, leave a note for others that you are on a call and not to be interrupted, and commit to listening fully.

HOW TO HAVE A CONVERSATION

How hard is it to have a conversation? Is talking to each other really something that human beings need to "learn" how to do? Celeste Head is the author of *We Need to Talk: How to Have Conversations That Matter*. In her book, she points out how the Buddha essentially said that if our mouths are open, we are not learning anything at all. Usually, when our mouths are open, what we are usually saying is some form of "me, me, me, all about me." Even when we think we're listening, we're not truly listening because we're thinking about what we should say next.

And then when you're on a video call, listening becomes all the more difficult due to a phenomenon known as "Zoom fatigue." How do you deal with that? How do you go about having an online conversation—versus an in-person one—especially when you're feeling Zoomed out? First let's be clear: Zoom fatigue is real. Psychologists say that too many video meetings exhaust us because our brains have to work significantly harder in a video format. We can't read nonverbal cues, we're staring at our own faces, and we're likely worried that an interruption will occur (the dog, the kid, a frozen screen, poor audio, you name it). We also don't get the warm, buzzy feeling that we can get from in-person meetings: walking to the conference room, friendly chitchat before the meeting commences, as well as side conversations and warm in-person facial cues or good old fashioned handshakes. When you're in an in-person meeting, you also can blend into the background when you're not speaking or presenting, but on a Zoom call, you're "on stage" the entire time, which can also exacerbate performance anxiety. When all of this is happening, it becomes even harder to listen because our senses are on overdrive. As Stephen Covey, author of *7 Habits of Highly Effective People*, said in his famous book, "Most of us don't listen with the intent to understand. We listen with the intent to reply." And whether you're meeting in person or on a video call, it really is that simple: take yourself out of the equation. (On Zoom you can do this literally by hiding your view of yourself.) I do this by repeating my mantra: *How can I help?* And when I am listening, really listening for *that* answer—a conversation naturally occurs. Because I lose focus on what *my* reply is going to be. When I am genuinely looking for the ways in which I can help, I am listening intently—and searching for that pattern, that constellation.

So the key to good conversations goes back to everything that Dr. Treasure said about listening. I know it's easier said than done because the ego tends to get in the way. But if you continually remind yourself to get into that receiving and absorbing mode—with practice, it gets easier.

CONNECT WITH FOUNTAINS, NOT DRAINS

Have you ever had the sense that some people spark energy in you—like a fountain—and others suck it away—like a drain? Especially IRL, as you gather among colleagues in meetings or where you share offices, pay attention to the energy you derive—or deplete—from each other. This interpersonal energy is called relational energy. Relational energy is that boost of positive energy you get—a surge of productivity, a feeling of competence—as a result of your interaction with someone else.[6] It's like a productivity high from a great connection. Studies have shown that this type of energy can boost the motivation and energy of others.[7] It is, essentially, contagious! Research has also shown that relational energy boosts things like resilience, resourcefulness, creativity, and productivity.[8] The good news is that relational energy—like listening—is a skill that can be honed. As Wayne Baker pointed out in an article in *Harvard*

Business Review, until somewhat recently collegial relationships were overlooked as a source of energy. But as he learned in research conducted with his colleagues Bradley Owens, Dana Sumpter, and Kim Cameron, our relationships with coworkers, colleagues, and clients impact our personal source of energy.[9]

When we are working—processing, analyzing, thinking deeply—we need energy. Pay attention to the people you're connected to and how they affect your supply: do you feel inspired by them? Or do you find yourself dragging after a meeting? Look also at the energy that you give off to others: Does your audience look alert or drained? Yawning? Are they falling asleep? Baker and his colleagues found in their research that there are four different ways interactions can be energizing: when we create a positive vision, when we contribute meaningfully to a conversation, when we are fully present and attentive, and when we have interactions that provide a sense of progress and hope. If you think about mentors, colleagues, and even friends who give you that positive buzz of energy and momentum, my guess is that your interactions with them mirror one—or perhaps all—of the preceding instances. And in that way, you can become a better source of energy for others by seeking to create inspiring visions, by adding to the dialogue in a way that adds value and meaning, by actively listening to the person you're talking to, and by making progress on whatever it is you're working on together. It's also a great exercise for your team, your office, and anyone you meet with regularly.

DON'T ISOLATE

Whatever issue it is that you want to discuss—philanthropy, food insecurity, environmental sustainability, and beyond—*you* can create necessary community by bringing people together. If you have a burning desire to solve one of the world's many challenges (and I hope you do)—get out there and gather the people needed to make that happen. Doing so will not only create a sense of relational energy, but it will circle back to feed you. My biweekly lunchtime corporate social responsibility chat (#CSRchat) series on Twitter was a great example of this. From 2010–2018, it brought people together to create a larger movement that really helped bring life to a nascent field of corporate social responsibility—which is inherently global and didn't lend itself to in-person meetings outside of large, impersonal conferences. Many different people—all spread out across the globe—were trying to figure things out on their own and working in silos. I decided to create a biweekly #CSRchat—which gave people a place to come together to share common challenges and learn from one another. I launched it in 2010, when there were many technology companies aligning to solve the issue of young children working in child labor for conflict minerals. At the time, I knew nothing about the issue and decided to put the questions I had out to Twitter and it grew from there. Twitter was a very different place back then, but the response was overwhelming. Instead of suffering in frustration for my lack of knowledge about conflict minerals or struggling to make significant headway on my own, it became a way to gather people (and many experts) who had knowledge on a particular subject matter. What emerged was a community of people on Twitter who were working in corporate responsibility, wanted to work in corporate responsibility, received funding from corporations, or were selling to people in the field, and we all learned and collaborate with each other in such a synergistic way that was amazing to witness.

Today you can execute this in myriad formats beyond Twitter: Facebook Live, Instagram Live, Zoom, Microsoft Teams, and Google Hangouts. These platforms bring people together online in an atmosphere that is more intimate and vibrant than a series of tweets. Those relationships I built are lasting; I still collaborate with many of those people today. Don't assume that people will think you're nuts if you sent a direct message (DM), a Tweet, or LinkedIn message and say "Hey, I'd like to discuss this issue." If they are passionate about the same issues you are—they won't. Chances are better that they will admire your tenacity, your proactiveness in bringing people together. It may be terrifying to you—like walking up to a person standing alone at a party—but chances are quite good that person will in fact be relieved. We tend to think everybody else already has their network "established" and doesn't want new connections—and I've found the opposite to be true. Even the most famous athletes or accomplished CEOs can feel nervous or insecure in a social setting.

BE THE REAL YOU

I love meeting people in real life, but some people don't. And that's fine, too. Some of the most accomplished people I know prefer less social stimulation. The most important thing is to just be you.

> Somebody once said to me, "Oh my gosh, you're really you online."
>
> I thought, "Well, who else would I be?"
>
> Another person once said, "Wow, you are so much smaller than I ever envisioned."
>
> To that I responded, "Did you think I was a wildebeest?"
>
> "No," she said, "but you have such a big personality."
>
> *Well, you can be tiny and still have a big personality!*

It's true that some people project a certain persona—like a social media avatar that doesn't accurately reflect who they are—professionally or personally. You don't have to share every intimate detail of your life, and you need to use discretion and common sense. But never hesitate to be true to who you are—and don't pretend to be someone you're not. And do not hesitate to be forthright and just tell people: I would like to get to know you. I do this all of the time, and most people are receptive to it.

Ann Shoket is the former editor in chief of *Seventeen* magazine and the author of *The Big Life: Embrace the Mess, Work Your Side Hustle, Find a Monumental Relationship, and Become the Badass Babe You Were Meant to Be.* When I asked her about building meaningful business connections, she told me that she'll never forget the way I just reached out to her and said, "I would love to get to know you." She said this about it: "It was so refreshing, nobody did that in my world before; no one just said, 'I would like to get to know you. I don't know where it's going to go, or what can we do for each other, but let's just have coffee.'" Shoket and I are now dear friends, and of course you can't reach out to everyone and have coffee with thousands of people (and you shouldn't; remember, the goal here is constellations, not a collection of random stars). But when you have an instinct or a similar passion—or even better, when you see someone so different from you in race, gender, and background—have the courage to say: Wow, I'm curious what life is like for that person. I wonder what it's like to walk in that person's shoes. In those instances, have a tea or coffee together—and find out.

THE BOTTOM LINE: WHICH MEDIUM FOR WHICH CONTACT?

As you continue to add to your constellation of contacts, you will begin to develop a knack for knowing which particular medium (IRL, Zoom, Phone call, or DM) is best in which instance and for which particular contact. Until then, here are a few suggestions to get you started, offering some scaffolding for knowing which particular venue is best.

IRL. Whenever possible, it's best to meet someone for the first time IRL. Smiles, interpersonal chemistry, eye contact, the friendly buzz of a new kinship—these subtleties are nearly impossible to replicate online. If you need to have an important negotiation or discussion, or if you are interviewing for a job, in person is also best. You can avoid awkward digital hangups or miscommunication.

Zoom. Presentations (that don't need much discussion), status updates for an ongoing client or partner, or a replacement for an in-person meeting that can't take place due to cost, travel challenges, or distance, a Zoom meeting works best. Video calls are also ideal for small group gatherings of people who couldn't normally easily get together. Perhaps you're in London and your other attendees are in on the east and west coasts of the United States: one call that spans nine hours of time change!

By phone. For regular check-ins with clients and colleagues, especially if you work remotely. As much as people tend to avoid connecting by phone today, it's the perfect way to follow up with someone you've met with previously in person or by Zoom. Notice the way that you can listen—and be heard—by phone.

Snail mail. Use the good old-fashioned postal service to reconnect with old ties. Send a thank-you note to a mentor who helped you out long ago. Send a "how have you been?" letter to an old colleague or college professor who you admire. For the new business relationships, use snail mail as an opportunity to express gratitude for favors: thank you for the job referral, thank you for reviewing my résumé—as I said, I always have stamps handy! Next time you go to ping someone on LinkedIn or via text, ask yourself if you could instead send a brief handwritten note.

THE CONSTELLATION EFFECT

I like to think of people as a storyboard, as a picture that is constantly evolving. When you build relationships that are not static, temporary, or limited to a particular project or venture—you never know what can emerge. Each person is a piece of a larger vision: for you, for them, and for global issues we face as a society. By now hopefully you are getting a sense of how the constellation analogy applies and how you can use it to cultivate your own relationships. There are synergies to appreciate and enjoy over the course of your professional career or even a lifetime. Your ideal contact isn't derived by asking, "Who do I know in marketing," for instance, but rather, "Who do I know that cares about helping people?" Or, "who do I know who cares about my line of work, or the particular mission or objective I'm trying to achieve?" The key is to not limit your outreach by job titles, professional experiences, or even geographic locations. Keep your mindset focused on your mission and your overall goals.

The question you should also be asking yourself isn't how do I build community and connections, but rather which ones should I focus on? Which communities should you join and which ones should you pass on? Which ones don't currently exist? Should you build that community? Or let someone else take the reins? In that sense, you don't need to worry about finding "that" investor, *the* perfect contact. Instead, worry about finding someone who simply cares about your mission and your values. When you do that, there is no shortage of creative ways to reach your ideal networking target through indirect contacts. Since we now know all the ways our existing contacts have value, why not tap them? Expanding your network through degrees of separation works. And when you have an inspiring mission and purpose—people will want to jump aboard.

ELEVATE YOUR OBJECTIVE

When you think about the type of constellation you want to create, it's helpful to have an objective with a lofty, inspiring vision. Rather than focusing solely on a small, short-term transaction: getting a job, securing a new partner, learning a new job-related skill, it's important to think about your highest ambitions. Let's say that in the near term, your goal is to get hired in an entry-level fundraising position. If you elevate your objective to: I want to eliminate world hunger, you can see how this not only might inspire you in your daily work, but will serve to create the types of meaningful connections that will be beneficial long term. This objective elevation is exactly what Paul van Zyl did with The Conduit, which serves as a home for those committed to improving the world by harnessing the power of creativity and entrepreneurship. Van Zyl's essential question was: How do you create a permanent community of people helping each other to use entrepreneurial solutions to tackle big problems? Van Zyl was very involved in the anti-apartheid movement, designed the structure and methodology of the Truth Commission, and also set up the International Center for Transitional Justice, which had over 200 staff and programs in over 30 countries helping nations deal with the legacy of human rights abuse. After he won the Skoll Award for Social Entrepreneurship, he was chosen as a Young Global Leader and started going to Davos, became a TED fellow, and spoke at events like the Aspen Ideas Festival and the World

Economic Forum. Van Zyl realized that these episodic gatherings were incredibly powerful, but that they also produced pockets full of business cards and failed promises to "see each other more often." The Conduit emerged as an attempt to build a more consistent ecosystem, where people trying to do what Van Zyl was doing could draw upon a community—investors, branding experts, and supply chain resources, for instance—all deployed toward a higher purpose. It became of hub for people trying to tackle ethical supply chains, decent work for people in developing economies, off-grid solar, or women's empowerment.

Instead of focusing on the granular and transactional problems that he wanted to solve, Van Zyl aimed higher with his mission and purpose and sought to create a community and a hub where a tremendous amount of great impact work could be done for the greater good. Whether you are in business development, sales, fundraising, technology—or any industry at all—there's always an opportunity to elevate your objective to a higher good. Even if you aren't in a position, or perhaps even interested in, creating a community the way that Van Zyl did, it can be helpful to participate in this type of thinking to figure out who you want—and should have—in your constellation. Instead of "get a job in public relations," think "use communications and media to eliminate gender bias" or whatever issue is important to you. When you move from the tactical to the inspirational, you will start to build a constellation that fuels both personal as well as professional growth.

IF YOU'RE A WOMAN, YOU NEED TWO NETWORKS

From pay wage gaps to gender biases to being overburdened with childcare and domestic responsibilities, women face myriad additional challenges in the workplace compared to men. As a result, women often feel as though they can only talk to other women about these particular problems, making it crucial that women have a separate network of other women for support. In fact, research from *Harvard Business Review* revealed why women need two separate networks—one that includes men, and then one that is female-only.[1] From their male network, women learn how to climb the corporate ladder and glean insights from male mentors. From their female network—especially with an inner circle of two to four women—women have a forum to talk about issues they might feel uncomfortable sharing with a man, like how a man stepped over them in a conversation, for example. The HBR study also found that women need a source of empathy and the ability to ideate off of that empathy with other women. Research also shows that women need to see examples of other women who have forged a way into leadership positions and understand how they can achieve that as well. A study published in the *Journal of Experimental Social Psychology* backs this up. In that study, women who saw images of successful, powerful women, like Hillary Clinton, before giving a speech outperformed their peers.

Jennifer DaSilva is president of the creative agency Berlin Cameron. She has spent the last 15 years managing key accounts like Coca-Cola, Heineken, Lexus, and Capital One. When she read about the research that pointed to the power of a female-only network and how women seeing other women in power could literally change immediate performance, she was inspired and saw an opportunity to create a constellation of connected women, aptly named Connect4Women. DaSilva wanted to create a community of women where they could experience that effect. In March 2019—since March is Women's History month—DaSilva made it a goal to connect four women each day in the hopes creating lasting connections and collaborations. Other women were inspired and joined in. The initiative became known as Connect4Women, and the community is open to anyone globally. DaSilva personally connected 500-plus women in 2019, which led to countless partnerships, business deals, new jobs, and friendships. It's been a surprising source of joy for DaSilva, especially during the throes of the pandemic when the need for connection and community became more profound—practically overnight.

WIE, an influential membership network and platform for women leaders, is another great example of the power of female networks. Dee Poku is an entrepreneur, a women's advocate, and a community builder and the founder and CEO of WIE. It began back in 2010 as the WIE Symposium—one of the early modern women's conferences, and was created partly in response to the lack of diversity at traditional business forums. In addition to providing its members with the community and tools to succeed in the workplace, WIE supports brands and corporations with their culture building and diversity initiatives. WIE has attracted numerous business and cultural leaders to its global gatherings, including Queen Rania, Melinda Gates, Mellody Hobson, Shan-Lyn Ma, Naomi Campbell, Arianna Huffington, Thasunda Duckett, Diane von Furstenberg, Nancy Pelosi, Katia Beauchamp, Dr. Jill Biden, Jennifer Hyman, Alek Wek, Katie Couric, Tyra Banks, Aileen Lee, Lauren Bush, Iman, Rosario Dawson, and Christy Turlington. From its initial spark of getting some of the biggest females in business together, WIE's mission transformed into a simpler cause of honing in on women and their careers and how they could learn from one another. And it all came back to that mission of helping women feel seen. Poku says:

> If you make a person feel seen, it does wonders. It doesn't matter who they are. They could be the most successful person in the world or a junior intern. If you make people feel seen, they will jump over rivers for you.

For WIE and for many other powerful networks like it, the strength of the community isn't really about the job titles, the bank accounts, or the companies that these women represent—it all boils down to the power of human authenticity, of shining a light on each other and offering a means to show up and be seen. And this is the constellation effect in action, too. When women come together in this way—through a constellation of supportive backers—they can not only cocreate new ideas and solve challenging problems but they can also elevate and amplify other women by their leadership and by displaying their power for other women to emulate.

NAIL YOUR STORY

Making an authentic connection with someone starts with laying the foundation, by figuring out how you might best fit together. A smart first move is to know your own story, your narrative—what skills you bring and where you're headed—like the back of your hand. Because once you do make those connections with others— perhaps even contact your ideal client or partner—what happens then? Once that connection transpires, you need to be ready to make the most of it. For that to happen, DaSilva says that you need to be prepared to tell your story. Your story should be yearning to come out of you. And if you can entice others to be as passionate about your story as you are, then the majority of your work is done. If you've elevated your mission to something audacious—a lofty mission that can change the world—it's easier to get people to want to jump aboard your train. Van Zyl did this to great effect with The Conduit. Once he created a community of people passionate about positive social change, he began gathering people around content, convenings, solutions, and capital. And when you build community in that intentional way, conscious about your mission and purpose—it's authentic. The Conduit is arranged around seven broad themes aligned with the big challenges the world is facing: climate, sustainability, economic opportunity, job creation, health, wellness, and nutrition. Then they began to develop the best possible content in accordance with those themes so that people could spend 10 percent of their time talking about the issue or problem and 90 percent of the time discussing the solution. How do you improve the status quo or lead to rapid system change? Then when the community comes together, it's for a clear and cohesive reason. And if you can build in what Van Zyl calls "stickiness" around that higher mission, a purpose and content, and then community and solutions will spring forth.

When you have a story like *that*—people who can help, will.

Distill your story down to its essence: What are you trying to accomplish? And how can you elevate your story into a mission that others can rally behind? When your story is polished and clear, it's significantly easier to figure out how you best fit with others— to create a constellation. Having a coherent story and adjusting it over time (in a rough draft, initially, and then later, into a polished version) clarifies not only your own mission, purpose, and potential—but also that of the constellation you want to create. And when everyone in your constellation is clear on their story, too, the collaboration and results that can spring forth can be profound.

FIND OUT HOW OTHER PEOPLE
FIT INTO YOUR STORY

Don't ever be afraid to ask someone who they know. As long as you are giving to a relationship as much as you are taking, it's perfectly fine—and even expected—to ask. Most people find connecting and helping others to be a source of joy and fulfillment—and you'll never know what you leave on the table if you don't ask. If you're uneasy about how to find out who knows who, take up some classic icebreaker techniques like sharing a factoid when you introduce yourself (even the *Fortune* Most Powerful Women Summit does this at their yearly conference). The more random and seemingly off-topic, the better!

When you've nailed down the essence of what you're trying to achieve, it's time to revisit any dormant ties: Do they fit into your constellation? Even if they don't, they might know someone who does. Or you might ideate off of an idea they share or something they are working on. When Shoket was researching her book *The Big Life*, she was fascinated at the ways that the women who gathered around her dinner table were aiming to support each other. She hosted dinner parties, which she called Badass Babes dinners. She would invite one woman and say, "Bring a friend of a friend of a friend." She hosted about two dozen dinners writing the book and another two dozen dinners across the country promoting the book, just watching the natural way that these women who didn't necessarily know each other didn't want to leave her house after sharing a cheese plate, some pizza, and a bottle of wine. Shoket was amazed at the way these women were organically supporting each other, since she didn't see that growing up in the business. As she said:

> I didn't see a lot of people who just wanted to be friends and to help each other. I saw a lot more competition among groups of colleagues in the same industry. I actually didn't realize fully the importance of my network until I was no longer in a traditional corporate environment. I had a long career moving up a traditional ladder at Hearst Magazines, which is a giant company. And the important relationships that I needed to nurture to continue to move ahead were built in. It was the executives who were a couple levels ahead of me, or in a different department that I was going to start working with. Which is also not to say that I didn't nurture those relationships, but they felt expected and easy. But when I left that job, I was able to see these more organic networks blossoming in my own life, that the women who no longer had to be in business with me, but wanted to be in business or wanted to be in my orbit because they thought what I was saying was interesting, or what I was doing was interesting.

The millennial women who are part of Shoket's Big Life network told her that they feel isolated and lonely at work because of the generational differences and that even more to the point, they also feel that social media is very isolating. They really suffer with this feeling of "everyone else's having fun except for me." And as much as they recognize that Instagram is the highlight reel, they also find themselves unable to consistently remind themselves of that fact.

But Shoket advocates for having a regular group of ambitious women who can help each other through some of the most complicated parts of navigating your own ambition and success. She suggests having a regular dinner—it can be hosting your own Badass Babes dinners—or just a regular group of women that you can tap for their resources, for their expertise. Sometimes you don't necessarily want to vent to your spouse, partner, or to your best friends. Sometimes you just want to be heard, you need to vent about the crap that's going on in your office and be listened to without judgment.

ADAPT AND CHANGE YOUR MISSION IN REAL TIME

Has your mission changed? Does it need to? Sometimes it changes and sometimes you have to change to accommodate the world. It's not unusual to have to adjust the mission of what you're trying to achieve, and often—unexpectedly. As I was conducting these interviews, we were one month into lockdowns and shelter in place orders to slow the spread of coronavirus. Every business was rapidly adjusting along with the rest of the entire world. When the pandemic hit as I was interviewing Van Zyl, The Conduit was experiencing a huge shift. They were ordered by the UK government to shut their doors. But what happened next was remarkable. The first thing Van Zyl asked was, "How do we serve our community?" They pivoted to do digital programming and webinars with over 15,000 participants. The second thing they did was to ask, "How do we think beyond ourselves and focus on who is most at risk?" In response to that question, they jumpstarted a program to deliver food to frontline NHS workers, healthcare professionals, and doctors, delivering 30,000 meals and 20,000 loaves of bread to the front line in three hospitals.

When you've established an elevated purpose and the world comes to a screeching halt—the people you need to reach your immediate goals might drastically change. But when you're clear on your mission, it's still relatively easy to get what you need to carry out your mission, and to do it quickly—especially when lives are on the line.

ASSESS YOUR ABILITY TO
DRAW DIVERSITY

Have you ever paused to assess the diversity in your professional network? Think about the people with whom you do business. Or if you're young and just launching your career—or even looking for your first job—consider the professionals you'd *like* to be in business with or those you are reaching out to in your job application or career outreach efforts. What are the age, gender, racial, socioeconomic, and geographic makeup of this group? Is a wide variety represented within each category? Take a moment to consider this now: How diverse is your network? Are there steps you could be taking to make it more likely that you draw a diverse crowd of people together around a shared goal? Authentic and diverse conversations enhance our personal and professional lives exponentially. Meeting people from different walks of life or experiences can give you valuable insights into how your company can better serve its existing audience or branch out into a new one; you might realize you had a service or talent you didn't know you had or didn't know was needed. Your connection might bear fruit sometime in the future, when you've reinvented your business or moved to a new place.

It may not be news to you that having a diverse network is a valuable asset, but what's less commonly understood is that similarity doesn't necessarily breed connection. You might think that by socializing or working among people who are "like you," you will be more likely to find connections and relationships that will evolve into a meaningful relationship. But in fact, that's not necessarily true. It's interesting to think about what makes connections stick.

Adam Grant is a psychologist and author of three bestselling books, including *Give and Take: Why Helping Others Drives Our Success.* As a professor at the Wharton School of the University of Pennsylvania, he specializes in organizational psychology. Grant says that similarity isn't always enough to spark a connection. "If just having something in common was enough for a bond, we'd feel immediate chemistry with everyone who grew up in our hometown or went to our high school," Grant says. "What really greases the wheels of relationships," he says, "is uncommon commonality—sharing something that's rare. It's the feeling you have when you meet someone in a foreign country who grew up in your hometown: when the similarity is uncommon, it feels special." It's the reason I connect so quickly with other women who lost their mothers tragically, as not everyone has experienced such a trauma. These connections tend to emerge organically, but it's useful to put yourself in as many situations as you can to diversify the depth and breadth of your experience.

GATHER REVIEW: WHAT WE'VE LEARNED

In the *Gather* section, we've covered suggestions, research, and insights about how to begin to develop—or continue to nourish—meaningful business relationships in your life. In a nutshell, the *Gather* stage (of the *Gather*, *Ask*, *Do* method) is the who, what, when, where, and how of establishing those initial connections. The who, of course, starts with you. After all, every relationship begins with *you*. So remember to establish that first: if you are willing to be completely yourself, to be brave, and to get uncomfortable (within reason, of course!), the constellation you seek to create will more easily fall into shape. As my parents beautifully modeled for me: work and life aren't separate.

Next, get super clear on which skills you bring, what your vision is for your career—and find out how other people fit into it. In other words, nail your story. This brings me to the rest of the who in your network: the other stars in your constellation. To create the most brilliant, meaningful, and effective constellation, proactively seek diversity, and find connectors who can further expand your reach, and if you're a woman—make sure you have a female-only network as well.

As far as *how* to connect: remember to keep it simple and start small. Use the contacts you already have, volunteer with organizations and causes you care about, find opportunities to preconnect or to serve as the host. (And if you can host a regular, ongoing gathering that can build organically—even better!) When it comes to the *where* to have your meeting, event, or gathering, again: keep it simple. A small, in-person breakfast meeting, a Zoom call, a quick snail mail note to reconnect with a dormant tie: what matters most is that you take action and make the connection happen. Don't overthink it: just keep adding to the constellation.

PART II
ASK

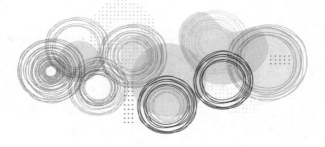

FOCUS: In this section, you will learn how to start connecting the dots (or stars) that you have gathered together in Part I. My method boils down to the most important ask of all: How can I help? But beyond that, we will also narrow in on how asking more (and the right) questions will begin to align the stars of your constellation into the pattern you want. Listening, speaking up, making the ask, and knowing how best to communicate in a world overexploding with communication tools will all be covered here. After all: How do you find out what someone needs? By asking them!

HOW CAN I HELP?

By now you've likely paused to think "how can I help?" when faced with a new connection or attending a new gathering. But the power and impact of these four simple words can go so much farther than that. By now, too, perhaps you've begun to see the power of building those constellations that I advocate. But when you become really skilled at asking "how can I help," the magnitude of the constellations that you can build and the great work they can create in this world are truly awe-inspiring.

When I meet someone for the first time, my first question after asking their name and chatting about something as simple as the food or drink being served is: "What is challenging right now, anything you need help with?" In some instances, this opening line is like a fast track to get you the precise *opposite* of what you really want. It might sound like you'll end up with a pile of work rather than help! However, these simple words have radically changed the course of my business endeavors, primarily because they are so unexpected. Reframing the classic "ask" to be nontransactional breaks down the barrier of quid pro quo that often stymies business relationships and makes networking events so unbearable. Most people dread conference room small talk because it feels superficial.

But the minute you ask someone how *you* can support them, their ears perk up. It also establishes equality. You no longer give off the impression of a desperate someone who needs something or is afraid of being perceived as lower on the professional totem pole. Instead, you tip the scale of power and control in your favor. By taking action, you establish yourself in a position to help, support, and guide.

HOW CAN I HELP YOU?

Imagine you're at an event where you don't know many people. You're wearing name tags, awkwardly eating food, and looking for a place to put down your drink. You engage in a meaningful conversation with someone about your line of business. Instead of rattling off your elevator pitch about what *you* bring, ask them, "What's challenging for you right now?" And listen. You will be amazed at what you learn. Think back to all of the business conversations you've had over the years when you *could* have asked those questions but didn't. Perhaps you missed an opportunity to help a colleague or a boss. Maybe you could have helped find someone a babysitter or fixed someone's laptop. The possibilities are endless.

Leading with "how can I help?" is effective because most people hesitate to lead from a position of weakness. But offering your help obliterates the notion of weakness altogether; it brings you and a potential client, colleague, or friend one step closer together. This conversation starter equalizes the room by reminding everyone: we all can benefit from assistance, care, and support. It also asserts your intentions: I have something to offer. At McPherson Strategies, we are in the business of helping clients improve communications around corporate social responsibility and social impact. Why not directly get down to the business of finding out what people need— instead of selling them on something they don't?

Asking "how can I help?" is an invitation for synergy. It sends the message: *I am interested in what you do and who you are.* Compare that to a networking conversation where someone is looking over your shoulder, eyeing an impressive founder, or looking past you toward a VP of company they'd die to work for. Which conversation will establish a better chance for doing business together in the future? You don't always have to ask business questions. This is obviously a tactic that needs to be used judiciously. I do not recommend circulating around the entire gathering, saying, "Hi, I'm Susan. How can I help?" on repeat. That would be irritating at best, disastrous at worst. Just shift your thought process. Before you walk into the room, pivot your internal monologue from "what can I be getting" to "what can I be offering?" Pick a few people with whom you feel a sense of synergy and make an offer to them. This shift in mindset will immediately put both you and the recipient, at ease. When someone offers to help *you*, it feels wonderful. An offer of help expresses far more than just exchanging business cards. (Or tapping your email address into their customer relationship management application.)

In my experience, offering to help gave me a strategic way to enter the conversation. It provided an avenue for significant learnings, connections, and in most cases—a return of the favor, too. I've also learned that *everybody* has something to give: an introduction, a recommendation letter for a child's school or a job application, an hour spent editing someone's LinkedIn profile. Every single person has a currency that they can offer, and you don't need permission or prestige to do so: it's a mindset.

You have something to offer, as well, no matter how small or insignificant it may seem to you. Take a moment to jot down a few things you could offer. You'll find yourself pleasantly surprised. Trust me.

I often ask people where they're from. Since I've lived so many places, it truly helps in finding a point of connection. But if we haven't lived in a similar place, I would ask, "I've always wanted to go there—what's it like?" (and then listen to the answer). I also often pause the conversation to make sure I've understood everything that person shared because learning more about our world is actually a gift. "Oh my gosh, can you repeat that?" I'll say and then jot it down or put it in my phone. Then when I go to follow up with that person, I have accurate details. Sometimes I even ask if I can take a picture of the person (not for sharing), so I can properly recall our conversation. And later, when I look at the notes after the event, I might have a light bulb moment: oh, Sheryl is from a western suburb of Chicago and so is Andrea, and they both are passionate about economic policy and dogs—I should introduce them.

HOW IT FUELS LEARNING

It is vitally important that we understand differing perspectives, for our business as well as our broader lives. Our country is in a deep polarization crisis: we don't understand people who we perceive to be different from us. Philosophically, it may be difficult to broker a conversation with someone whose political, social, and environmental views are so vastly different from our own. But listening fuels *understanding*. And if you want to succeed in business, you will be infinitely more successful if you deeply understand everything you possibly can about your industry, the people in it, and the major problems that need solving. Engage a curious mindset: What does this person in front of you know that you don't? It doesn't matter who they are—they know something (likely, a lot of things) that you don't. And if you can absorb that knowledge, you'll be more informed, better educated, and well-rounded. What could you learn from their perspective? Even if you don't agree with it or if it isn't directly applicable to your job, is there something you can take away from this exchange of information and ideas? If it's a colleague—even if you're not working in the same department or on the same projects: What's on their mind? What could you learn from each other? If you're in sales, you should be asking your colleagues in operations what's hard for them and how you could help. Why? You're going to be a better salesperson because you're going to be able to explain to your client or your customer why your company is the better choice when you have a comprehensive view of the entire organization.

WHAT EXPERTISE OR EXPERIENCE DO YOU HAVE TO OFFER?

Whether it's considering which job you should apply for or pausing to think about which next step you want to take in your career trajectory, many if not most of us start the process by considering what we *want*. Which company or organization we want to work for, which position we want, what level of salary we desire—and if we're not careful—our want list becomes much too detailed and long. There's nothing wrong with wanting a fantastic career, whatever that means to you. But pausing to consider which particular skills and experience you have to offer is a different way to look at your career—and the people in it—and is an approach that I've also seen work quite effectively.

Shiza Shahid is a Pakistani social entrepreneur, social activist, investor, and educator. She is the cofounder and former CEO of the nonprofit Malala Fund, which promotes education for every girl, and now the cofounder and CEO of Our Place, a cookware brand for the modern, multiethnic American kitchen. Her work illustrates how asking "How can I help?" will not only connect you with people—but it will also tightly align you with your passion and purpose. Shahid and her husband are both immigrants. She grew up in Pakistan, he grew up in Iran—and both are passionate about building communities by gathering. Shahid says she's made a practice of hosting gatherings to connect guests across cultures around a dinner table. When she noticed there wasn't a kitchenware brand that celebrated global culture and connection—she and her husband decided to create one.

"Nothing connects us like home cooking does," Shahid says. "It is the most connecting force there is in the world." Shahid says that most of our happiest memories are around some kind of home-cooked meal or eating and gathering at home—it's the bedrock of culture, which can sometimes slip away. Being from Pakistan, she notices that sometimes she doesn't wear Pakistani clothes as often or speaks more English than she does Urdu. But if you arrive in her kitchen, you will immediately sense her Pakistani culture and heritage. She and her husband created Our Place to make products that make it easier to cook at home so you can better connect to your body and health as well as food systems, farmers, community, and family, as well as friends and traditions. But starting Our Place isn't the first time that Shahid has asked "how can I help" and created something remarkable out of the answer. Shahid says, "When it feels like I'm perhaps the only person who can do something, I tend to just do it."

At 19, Shahid met Malala Yousafzai, who was then 11—they became fast friends. Three years later, Malala was shot. At that time, Shahid felt like she was the only person who might be able to translate the tragedy of Malala's courage into something that could inspire positive good and action. Shahid was 22 and working at McKinsey. The idea of leaving the stability of that job at such a very young age to try to build an organization around a girl who was shot in Pakistan at the age of 14, was, in her words, "a completely irrational thing to do." And yet for her it wasn't a question. She went on to cofound and serve as CEO of the Malala Fund.

It all started with that question: *How can I help?*

Executing a "how can I help" mindset is crucial. It's often the exact opposite of our internal monologue. It's easy to revert back to the "what will I get" or "what's in it for me" thought process that so often dominates workplace culture. But if you think about it, your work, your career, your vocation isn't really meant to serve you. Of course, it does in many ways—income, meaning, purpose, and above all relationships. But when you think about your "life's work," I hope that in some way what you choose to do with your one precious life will serve others, will somehow leave this world better than it was when you arrived in it. Asking yourself *those* kinds of questions can activate an offering mindset: What do I have that can benefit others?

Susan Danziger is another CEO and founder who has built business and social impact organizations—and a brilliantly successful career—just by pausing to ask the question *how can I help?* She says that when she gets an answer, she iterates on that response, using it as a way to self-reflect and ask: No, really—how *can* I help? As in what unique skills and expertise do *I have* that I can skillfully bring to business—or societal—problems that need solving? Most recently, Danziger created The Spark of Hudson, a learning center in the town of Hudson, New York, working to solve the issues of poverty within its borders. On a per capita basis, Hudson is the third largest creative community in the United States: writers, artists, craftsmen, all live there. With a population of about 6,000—Hudson has an economically stratified community: one-third of the population is quite well off, one-third are middle class, and one-third live at or below the poverty line. The Spark of Hudson boasts 10,000 square feet of workforce development and training facilities as well as a cafe for community, a classroom, an events space, and rooms to stay overnight during classes. As Danzinger says,

> I realized that by opening a center where people learn together, I could supercharge my connecting skills. The Spark is all about bringing people together and making connections, with or without my being there. In effect, it's a way to scale connections: a space where others can gather, connect and learn from one another. My hope is that in the town of Hudson, which has been quite divided, The Spark will help people understand and appreciate one another.

First, The Spark of Hudson works with people in the community to figure out what career they are interested in—then they are matched with short training courses and placed into paid internships that put those skills immediately to use.

When I interviewed Danziger for this book, we were about five weeks into shelter in place during the lockdown to slow the coronavirus. And what she had done to help people in need—to literally bring the "how can I help" ethos to fruition—in that short span of time was nothing short of remarkable. The Spark of Hudson fed healthcare workers and spearheaded an initiative to support the restaurants. People donated to restaurants, which kept them in business, and then they provided those meals to hospital workers. This program has now evolved into Feed Hudson: people donate to restaurants to feed the most vulnerable elderly people living in low-income housing. They also offered emergency grants of $500 to over 60 families, with plans to extend to undocumented workers. Students from 50 local families didn't have access to the Internet and couldn't attend school—but within a few days, Danziger arranged a telephone company to send 50 phones to these families to act as hotspots. She's also partnering with Andrew Yang to execute a universal basic income (UBI) pilot so that for five years, people will receive a guaranteed $500 per month.

All of these efforts are created to help reverse the cycle of poverty. It shows promise for becoming a case study in what communities around the globe can do to intervene and break this perpetual cycle. When I asked Danziger what she thought about how to execute the "how can I help" mindset, she said there are two ways she sees it. First, some people are innate givers, and for them, the notion of "how can I help" will likely emerge organically. But for others—who aren't necessarily aligned with that mindset—you can be a bit more strategic. Establishing yourself as someone who convenes stakeholders, key influencers, and interesting individuals offers you the ability to meet the people you want *and* gives you credibility to establish a genuine rapport.

The cofounders of the organization Modern Loss created their project in a similar way. Cofounders Rebecca Soffer and Gabrielle Birkner met shortly after Rebecca's mom was killed in a car accident on Labor Day in 2006. Four years later, her father died from a heart attack. The two future cofounders met when a mutual friend invited a few people who had all lost a parent to dinner. Birkner had also lost her dad and her step-mom—and the two quickly bonded over their shared losses and grief, and developed a quick friendship. The two said that with other friends and colleagues, they found conversations about grief to be challenging. They often found that people would try to fix their problem, offer unhelpful platitudes, or even just ignore them completely.

When I asked Soffer how Modern Loss was established from that ethos of "how can I help," here's what she said:

> I had gotten increasingly sick of how we address grief in our society, and specifically how we *don't* address grief, which is through platforms that are more casual, more inviting, involve

some humor, point toward resilience and living a high-quality life not just in spite of but sometimes because of your loss, and offer zero judgment on how you're moving through your loss, as long as you aren't hurting yourself or anyone else. I was also quite tired of not having anywhere to go to explore and consider grief outside of the obvious go-tos, such as therapy. Modern Loss came from a desire to build a community and to offer both peer-to-peer and shared stories, because we're both storytellers.

And so from their shared pain—further compounded by the additional pain of grief and with all of the challenges that our culture has inadequately addressed—Modern Loss was born. From a desire to help others going through a similar experience, a life's work and a career purpose was found, and as a result, hundreds of thousands of people have been able to find healing and support that they otherwise might not have received.

Our Place, The Spark of Hudson, and Modern Loss were all created by founders who used their personal experiences—and in some cases, the pain of personal loss—to create something new: a line of cookware, a community for shared grief, a hub for in-person learning and connection to bridge cultural and economic divides. Three very different businesses—but each of these founders had an aha moment about what they had to offer, which skills and expertise they could use to help others. Even if you don't wish to be an entrepreneur or have any desire in creating your own business, this mindset can be quite helpful.

Ask yourself: What expertise do you have that others find valuable? What advice do friends, family members, or colleagues come to you for? What are the skills that you have that could bring the most value to your colleagues and connections? What do you excel at? Even if the answers to these questions don't induce your own aha moment overnight, keeping them top of mind over time will create the type of reflection and self-awareness that brings you further in the constellation in which you belong.

HELP TO DISSOLVE FEAR OF FAILURE

As human beings we all have insecurities that lead to a fear of being judged. When it comes to connecting—or doing anything, really—imagining all the ways that we can fail can cause us to want to quit before we've even started. And this is another way how the helping mindset takes the edge off. When people act out of fear or feel nervous that other people are judging them—when they think, "Oh my God, what if it doesn't work?"—they might freeze or give up and quit, and that prohibits people from taking risks. However, when you become a convener, the risk lessens. When your goal is helping, failure isn't really an option. Even if you've helped *a little*—that is a win. When Danziger started DailyLit, a digital publisher, the traditional publishers weren't going digital yet. And at the time she was thinking: How do I figure out a way to land my first customer? Instead of giving up, she took initiative and created Publishing Point, where she would convene gatherings once a month, invite a speaker, and open it up to those working in publishing. She launched a Meetup and started securing incredible speakers: company CEOs and professionals from every major trade house, the founder of FourSquare, the founder of Twitter, and others commanding influence. Doing this gave her a seat at the table. Remember what we learned in the *Gather* section? When you're the host, you can bring the people you want to your table in a much less threatening way, and it can create tremendous value for all in a way that offers help, kindness, and genuine support.

But wait—can't being a giver put you in a position to be a doormat? If executed poorly couldn't you possibly get taken advantage of? Where is the line between giving too much versus too little? Adam Grant says that being a giver doesn't mean saying yes to every request. Instead, he proposes, it means setting boundaries around who, when, and how you help. The *who* is about setting boundaries with takers—if someone has a history or reputation of selfish behavior, you're not obligated to help. If you give to people who tend to be generous or fair, you avoid rewarding the wrong behavior and invest in spreading norms of generosity. The *when* is about setting boundaries with time. Failed givers drop everything whenever they get a request; successful givers block out time for their own goals and for self-care. The *how* is about setting boundaries with the types of help you give. The idea is to be what he calls a "generosity specialist": help in ways that *energize* you rather than *exhaust* you, and in situations where you can add unique value. He also recommends what he calls "the five-minute favor," which are high-benefit, low-cost giving favors such as sharing knowledge and making introductions. It makes his day when he's able to share ideas and evidence in the realm of work and psychology or connect people who benefit from knowing one another. Grant also says that when you have impressive skills, a project that you've worked hard on and produced a solid outcome, people will want to connect with you and you don't have to schmooze. When you have something to offer beyond "I want to network," the proof is in the pudding, so to speak, and your work speaks for you.

Many people start by asking *that* question and it leads to an entire new venture, social enterprise, or nonprofit organization. There are a lot of problems out there that need solving: business and otherwise. But if you walked into a room and firehosed your résumé in someone's face and blabbed their ear off about what you need and what you're doing, what would you learn? I won't tell you that you'll learn absolutely nothing, but I can tell you that it will certainly be less fruitful.

The bottom line—asking "how can I help?" will always point you in the right direction. Whether you are asking "how can I help in this moment" or "how can I help in this life"—listen to those answers. Those answers are the key to finding your path, your constellation, and the people who will see you and help you feel most seen.

KNOW YOUR ASK: THE WHO, WHAT, WHERE OF GETTING WHAT YOU WANT

Abraham Lincoln famously said, "Give me six hours to chop down a tree, and I will spend the first four hours sharpening the ax." This concept of skilled preparation is true in building effective business relationships, too. Those first proverbial four hours are best spent cultivating the connection—building trusted allies. Then with an entourage of supporters who now share your vision and passion (a sharp ax, rather than dull), you are poised to accomplish your goal. In this scenario, the dull ax is the equivalent of a weak LinkedIn connection or a passing acquaintance you once traded business cards with at an event. With a dull blade like that, you might whack for six hours, only to find that tree still standing despite best efforts.

Perhaps you've been making deeper business connections using the tools that you have learned in this book. Maybe you've crystallized your offering so you're in a better position to ask for what you want from a specific person—and get it. But the artistry in the art of connecting is that it's a constant evolution—one that never ends.

True connections never finish or reach the completion of the ask phase of the relationship. A connection that ends after the ask is not a connection. It's a business transaction. These phases are all interwoven and intertwined. You're consistently deepening the connections that you have, building new ones, and tending to dormant ones, too. And in that way, the asks will unfold organically. Of course, there will be instances in which you will make a big ask, perhaps in a boardroom with a transition plan for your company, and impeccable, practiced preparation. But the best connectors make micro-connections and mini-asks and gives along the way, finding themselves with a sharpened ax—better positioned and prepared to nail a big ask when the time is right. Most pursuits require preparation, and making an ask is no exception.

PREPARE YOUR OSCARS INTRO

Ladies and Gentleman, I'm honored to introduce . . .

At the Oscars, or any awards ceremony, the recipient receives a warm introduction before they take the stage. It typically includes a two-minute spiel of that person's life or accolades along with a bit of humor and levity. When you're preparing for a meeting, do you research as though you were preparing an Oscars intro for that person? With digital sleuthing and research tools abound, there's no excuse not to have their bio down. Ask yourself: Could I stand up to introduce this person, and hit their key five data points? The key five are age, school, passion projects, media, and company news. Nothing will impress someone more—or better convey how closely you're paying attention—than if you can walk in and say, "I saw you funded the ACLU today with an incredible gift. Congratulations and thank you!" LinkedIn, Twitter, and good old-fashioned Google will serve this information up in a few clicks. Have they written articles? If so, read them and prepare a follow-up question: "What did you mean when you said that Slack would change the way you do business?"

Once you've nailed your Oscars intro (you know their bio and five key data points by heart), add some color to your intel by widening the frame of your research. Have you talked to everyone who knows that person? Many people make the assumption—an oversight—that relationships are two-way: what you can do for me and what I can do for you. But there are infinite layers of connection and collaboration. Perhaps the ask you have in mind isn't even the best one for a synergistic business outcome for you both—so do the legwork, come prepared with a 360-degree view, with as many details on the multilayered facets of this person as you can.

HANDSHAKE OR HUG?

Now that you've done all of your homework on *who* they are and *what* they've done, your job now is to consider *how* they may like to interact. Some colleagues are huggers. Others are hand shakers, and at the present time with COVID-19, some prefer phone, others Zoom, others text. Consider the geographic, social, and ethnic backgrounds of who you are meeting. The way that you build rapport with a 65-year-old board member in New York is very different than the way you will connect with a 26-year-old actress in Los Angeles. The way you build a relationship with someone in Michigan might be different than the way you would do it in Florida or Italy or Japan. It's a dance—on the one hand, you're building the relationship, but ultimately, the person knows you're going to ask them for business, a quote, or a donation. It's often two steps to the right (getting to know each other as human beings) and two steps to the left (conducting business). Depending on that person's cultural background, the dance may move faster, slower, or to a different beat. Stay attuned and let them set the pace.

My mentor Nancy Sells was senior VP of sales at PR Newswire and has a decades-long career as a master in sales and now conducts sales trainings globally. She was once teaching a training course for professionals selling home loans over the phone. During a discussion about different strategies to connect with clients on a human level on the telephone, one of her students told her, "Nancy, I don't care where their kids went to school." He said that in his culture, it just wasn't something people did. This is an important distinction to observe. But when Nancy pointed out that being able to bond as human beings over the phone was an essential sales tool, the student wanted to learn how to do it more effectively. I include this example as a reminder that every culture has different norms and expectations around connecting interpersonally. When you are making connections, be mindful of this. If you're pitching or selling to someone who is a bit more guarded or closed off, or from a different culture, be sensitive to that. Listen to their cues, pay attention to their reactions, and don't push. If you make a mistake, apologize and move on. A business relationship is like any other relationship and should never be forced.

Connection is as much a learned skill as playing the violin or scoring a goal in soccer. We *all* have the ability to connect around humanity and the experience of being alive. But it is important to note that some people do this more naturally. For those who don't, I prefer to say they don't *yet*.

THE THREE COMPONENTS
OF BUILDING TRUST

Once you've ironed out your mission, business plan, or job search agenda—and you know what you want to achieve—you'll want to start folding people into your mission. But how do you do *that*? In a best-case scenario, the people you need help from are already involved and invested. And if they aren't yet—you need to make them aware of what you're doing and then get them involved. Later you will ask them to take action. But first, build awareness, engagement, and trust. Trust is built slowly, one coffee, one Tweet, one conversation at a time. It takes a long time to develop but can disappear in an instant.

Research from PricewaterhouseCoopers reveals that trust in business comes down to three essential elements: *competence, experience*, and *values*.[1] Before you get to the point of making an ask, your potential partner or client needs to trust you. They need to know that you do what you say you will, you keep promises, and you believe in the same values. Small actions over time—mini-deposits into each of these accounts—will build trust.

Just as differing cultures have different social norms on how they connect and build business relationships, cultural differences exist in norms around trust, too. For example, research conducted by *Harvard Business Review* found that participants they studied in North American and European cultures tended to have openness, meaning that they assume clients and partners are reliable and trustworthy until proven otherwise.[2] On average, people from those cultures tended to test for openness and value transparency as a signal of trust. That same study found that participants from East Asian cultures primarily valued competence. In business relationships, they tended to rely heavily on reputation and commonly tested for competence to gain trust. The study also found that participants from Middle Eastern and South Asian cultures indicated a preference for socializing before negotiating; they also placed a premium on assessing respect. The Latin American participants prioritized common values and also preferred socializing before negotiation. None of these findings are meant to suggest sweeping generalizations about how cultural differences influence business relationships. But the research is simply a mere peek into the different types of styles and approaches that you may find in business.

One action that will always endear trust: closing the loop. If someone made an introduction for you, say, for example, with a chief marketing officer of a Fortune 100 company in Chicago for a job interview—follow up and tell them what happened. Let them know how it went. Thank them with an email or a card. (You'd be surprised how many times this *doesn't* happen!) As you develop the art of connecting, you're also planting the seed for another reason to talk to that person. Each time you follow up and reconnect—they will notice. They will remember: this person is trustworthy, contentious. Your reputation is built over thousands of tiny little actions—showing up, small asks, offers, and loops closed—throughout your career.

THE FIVE-MINUTE ASK

When you're starting a new business or organization, instead of waiting until everything's ready to launch and *then* getting supporters—you want the reverse. You want supporters *early on* so that they can accrue a vested interest in it. The same is true of making connections in a job search process. Your greatest references for a dream job, customers for a new business, or supporters for a local campaign you care about will not necessarily be the ones who give you the most of anything, but the ones who are personally invested in your mission. Don't wait until you need a big ask before bringing in help. Use what I call the *five-minute ask*. There are a million different ways you could get specific help in a brief amount of time: What do you think of this business proposal? Could you retweet the details of this event? Could I get five minutes of your time to look over my résumé? Could you recommend the best technology platform to host my virtual summit? Can you offer some tips into breaking into the industry?

In his work as global head of community at Airbnb, Douglas Atkin often spoke about how and why people get incredibly passionate about certain brands and communities and not others. Why do some brands get a cultlike following, while others struggle to become a household name or even to stay in business? Atkin is also the author of the book *The Cult of Brands,* and he says that when brands build a cultlike following, it's because they've tapped into the human desire to belong. Humans want to belong to *something*. Atkins also touts the effective use of what's called the commitment curve to engage customers, investors, or community members. The commitment curve is a model that enables you to make asks of your community, volunteers, or potential customers over time. It illustrates how relationships deepen over time, with participants becoming increasingly committed to one another. The curve moves to the right, on the horizontal axis measuring time, and up along the vertical axis measuring commitment. As many have noted, it's like dating. You start with small, low-commitment asks: Would you like to get a coffee? And slowly build to larger ones: Would you like to marry me? And in between, there's a careful dance of engagement. What's fascinating is that Atkin and others who have used this model have found that the more someone does for your organization, the more invested they feel, the greater their sense of engagement and belonging. When you're at the beginning of the relationship: small, five-minute offers and asks are the way to begin.

11 QUESTIONS TO BREAK THE ICE

Let's say you've prepared your Oscars introduction, you've studied up on your contact's background, and you have some five-minute asks and offers in your arsenal. When you're about to meet face-to-face for a meeting, it's good to have some questions lined up, too. What will you talk about if you have already learned everything there is to know about them? Here are a few of my favorites to kick off any conversation, and notice none end with a yes or no answer.

1. What are you most interested in right now?
2. What's the last great meal you've had?
3. Where do your kids go to school?
4. Where in Brooklyn did your sister live?
5. Where are you from?
6. What gets you most excited right now?
7. What are you most curious about in the current world?
8. When you're not working, what keeps you busy?
9. What do you wish you had more time for?
10. What article or book have you read (or podcast have you listened to) or movie you have seen that I should check out?
11. If you could visit anywhere in the world next week, where would you go?

People love to talk about their kids. (And as a dog owner without kids, I love to share stories about my rescue pup, Phoebe.) But I find that it's helpful to have a few more questions in my back pocket to keep the conversation moving. You'll be amazed at what you can learn about people when you start asking lots of questions—and then actually, listen.

THREE OPTIONS FOR *YES*

Most people *want* to say *yes* and help you with your professional and personal goals. If you give people very prescriptive ways to do that—and multiple opportunities to say *yes*, they will respond. I suggest offering at least three different options for each ask. Let's say that you're looking for a new job. Option one could be forwarding your résumé on to three people in their network who could help you, option two could be agreeing to be a reference, and option three could be introducing you to one contact at a desired prospective company. For a fundraising ask, option one could be a donation, option two could be forwarding the opportunity to three other people who might be able to fund, and option three could be sending a tweet or posting on LinkedIn or Instagram. When given several options like this, most people will respond in some way. I serve on multiple nonprofit boards and often have to raise money as a member. But I realize that sometimes, a potential donor might be flushed with cash and in a position to give, but at other times they may be going through a rough patch and can't give as freely. Offering multiple options gives people the opportunity *not* to ghost you. Ghosting tends to happen when there's only one ask, and people are fearful to write back and say, "No, I can't." I'd rather have *some* response than none. When you get ghosted, you think, "Oh my God. Did I anger or upset them?" Instead, make it easier—and more comfortable—to say yes by offering three (or more) different ways to do that.

Sometimes, of course, there will be times when someone is leading you along on the road to nowhere, and nothing is happening. The old tire kicker—that person who always says they will do something for you but never does. And it's fine to be vulnerable and honest with that person, too. You can say something like, "We've been hanging out for two years, and I just love spending time with you. But are you ever going to introduce me to your CEO?" You have to find the right moment to do that, of course. But it's essential to get clear. You can't be in business with everyone, and it's better to know where you stand.

THE BOTTOM LINE

The word *ask* can make even the most skilled sales executive feel uncomfortable. But as we've learned in this chapter, asking for anything—whether it's an interview, a job, a promotion, or a donation to a cause you care about—is a natural step in most meaningful relationships. That's why the chapter on knowing your ask includes tips on deepening your business relationships: building trust, getting to know your constellation contacts better. As you move through the *Gather, Ask, Do* method, I recommend that you never stop the most important ask of all: asking questions. Once you do reach a point in the relationship where you are ready to ask for something, keep in mind ways that you can make things easier for the person on the receiving end of your request. If you can make it easy for them to say yes—either by giving them options (three options for yes!) or by making the request seem incredibly easy (the five-minute favor), you're much more likely to not only get what you want but also to deepen the relationship as both of you will walk away feeling happy.

PITCH PERFECT

Crafting your elevator pitch can arouse fear and dread in even the most prepared and poised people. But doing so is key to being able to discuss your work in *any* context, whether it's a dinner party, in line at the grocery store, on your favorite social media channel, or at a CEO roundtable.

ANNIHILATE ASKS ALTOGETHER

You've been reaching out to your contacts and have the perfect person to pitch or have started writing that ideal cover letter for that dream job. Or maybe you've been skillfully requesting the five-minute favor and have a perfect list of potential partners to contact. Maybe you need to hire a team member or find a producer for a television show or podcast you want to create. Perhaps you've got the ideal line of people set up to ask. But maybe, you don't need to make the ask at all. In some cases, yes, the ask *is* what you need. But it's worth asking yourself if you're following a set of rules, procedures, and approvals that you think you need, when really what you need isn't permission or funding but courage and scrappiness. Baratunde Thurston is a writer, comedian, commentator, and author of the book *How to Be Black*. He says that on a Saturday after he took his last flight back to California from New York before lockdown in March 2020, he woke up with three words in his head: live on lockdown. He wanted to make an entertaining, interactive, and participatory show about the pandemic that was informative and fun and also driven by the people who are in it—in the audience. Had he not been quarantined at the time, he would have put the wheels in motion to get all of the right approvals and people, funding, production, and hair and makeup. But since none of that was possible, he just started making the show. And people loved it. Instead of waiting for all the right pieces to fall into place—he just did it. From that experience, he developed excellent technical skills: editing video, sound, and imagery and all sorts of things he hadn't done in a very long time. A pandemic and lockdown situation will force you to be scrappy and innovate like that—but it's worth asking yourself every time. Does the "ask" you're dreaming of really need to happen? Could you bootstrap a solution and take immediate action that might push you to learn and innovate? Thurston said, "In six weeks, I did more publicly because of a pandemic than I did over the previous four years waiting for approval from some executive." Don't get trapped in limiting your thoughts or beliefs; ask yourself tough questions about whether or not the ask needs to happen in the first place.

Now of course if you're fresh out of college or new to the workforce, this gutsy approach might not make sense for you right away. Thurston was able to create a successful show because of the experiences he'd had and expertise he'd developed throughout his career. But even if you're new to the workplace, it's helpful to keep a disruptive mindset. The corporate ladder as we know it is disintegrating, and many of the *shoulds* and *musts* in the workplace are in our minds alone. I'd never suggest that you forgo valuable work experience right out of college or early on in your career—but what I do suggest is considering whether you need permission for passion projects or for taking on a new challenge that fuels your soul.

NAIL YOUR 4/4/4

For those asks that do need to occur, how do you handle them? What are the best tactics for making the ask? What about factors like urgency—do you need someone to do social media marketing today or can that wait until next week? Do you need someone to forward your résumé today, or is it your pool of references that need urgent attention? Do you introduce yourself at a large conference, where business cards are flying, or do you send a personal email and ask someone to lunch or coffee? Do you have the funds to offer someone compensation, or can you offer a trade of services?

First, I suggest you nail what I call the 4/4/4. First, your bigger vision, which you should always be thinking about: What do you need in *four years*? Next, what are your priorities for the next *four months*? Then bring it back to the next *four weeks* (or even four days). What's most critical? When you're making an ask: be very clear in what you want before you even step into the room, send an email, or make a call. And once there, be abundantly clear in stating it. If your long-term goal is to eliminate poverty, always have that at the forefront of your mind. How could this person help me achieve that goal? Where could they fit in?

LOOK FROM THE OUTSIDE IN

How does the world see you? Whether you are stepping into a conference room to meet a potential new employer or logging into an online meeting to make a sales presentation, it would be unrealistic to say that the world is impervious to how you look, sound, or present yourself.

As for me: I'm tiny. Thurston says that the world takes in people's demands, depending on who they are. A petite woman like me might get a different response than a man who is six foot three with a deep voice. That's not necessarily fair or right, but it's just reality. Some people may listen to a man standing at six feet three inches with a deep voice and think: he deserves to get what he wants because—listen to that voice!—even if it's over video. If the same request came from a woman, it might be perceived as arrogant or overly ambitious. So yes, you need to be honest about what your needs are and what your ask really is—but it's overly simplistic to shove gender, race, and other defining factors of your personality under the rug. The truth is that you will be perceived in a certain way, and it may not always be in your best interest or lead to the best outcome if you are always 100 percent honest about your ask. So yes, ask clearly for what you want, but do so skillfully and with grace.

Thurston says there is a temptation to think you know something once you've done it or read about it. The same is true of making asks or of any relationship-building skill. You're never at full mastery. You have to practice it—over and over and over. Think about how a friend might perceive your request for a favor and try it. Were you right? Ask someone in a volunteer capacity to give something. Role-play with a colleague or even in front of the mirror—there are a million different ways that you can practice. You'll screw up sometimes. That's OK. Ask your cousin. Ask your dog. Ask your neighbor. Just practice it.

ASSUME THE YES

How many times have you walked into a meeting where you hoped to get a *yes* (yes, you're hired; yes, you can have the budget you requested; yes, you can go on the trip and make the presentation to the board) with the assumption that you would get it? Whether it was asking your parents if you could take the car out when you were 16, or asking for a promotion at work—more times than not, we tend to anticipate and visualize rejection. But what would happen if we assumed that we'd get a positive response? Rhonesha Byng is CEO and founder of Her Agenda, an award-winning digital media platform bridging the gap between ambition and achievement for millennial women. When she was about 15, Byng realized that her purpose in life was to be a storyteller. But she didn't wait for permission or adulthood to get started. She just thought, "Well, I want to be a journalist; I'm going to reach out to this celebrity and ask for an interview." Byng grew up surrounded by powerful women in business: publicists, editors, media executives. It never occurred to her that most women get stuck in middle management and don't get into positions of power. "Wait," she thought, "there are only 20-something Fortune 500 CEOs who are female?" And then she realized: *you can't be what you can't see.* She decided to build Her Agenda. She realized that her contribution to creating more powerful women would include not only becoming one herself but also showcasing powerful women. Her goal was simple: she wanted people like Beyoncé's publicist or Valeisha Butterfield, chief diversity officer for the Recording Academy, to be every bit as well-known as Beyoncé herself.

As Dr. Treasure pointed out in his research on listening, the *way* you ask matters. How you speak impacts how your request is heard and responded to. If the ask is "I know I'm only 15, but I was just wondering . . ." it will be received very differently than "I'm Rhonesha, and I want to showcase you and share your story, do you have 15 minutes?" Your ask should also be specific, measurable, and time-bound: What exactly are you asking them to do and by what date? "Could you review my cover letter by next Friday?" "Could you lend 10 minutes of your expertise and hear my elevator pitch?" These are all pretty simple asks that someone could execute without having to put too much time and effort forth. Whatever your ask is and however you deliver it, be assertive in communicating what you want. In her book *Stop Playing Safe,* Margie Warrell suggests thinking about what your ideal outcome would be and then "confidently and courageously asking for it in a way that conveys you know your worth."

There's a quid pro quo in business, and everybody knows it. But the authenticity you've developed in your relationships lets you have the confidence to say, "It feels like we're a good fit." By the time you ask for someone to offer you the job, buy your product, or sign on as your client—whatever it is you need—it should feel natural. If you can position it that way, it never comes off as salesy, insincere, or desperate. At the end of an interview or meeting—if you've been skillfully getting to know the other person, absorbing what they say, and figuring out how you fit together into a constellation—it shouldn't feel uncomfortable to say, "Would you like to be in business together?" Cindi Leive is a media leader, journalist, and longtime advocate for women. She was the editor in chief of *Glamour* as well as *Self* magazine and a contributor to the *New York Times* bestseller *Together We Rise*, chronicling the making of the March for Women's lives. And she says that when it's time to make the ask, especially for women, "you should do so clearly and boldly and without apology." But she notes that while women in particular should never fall into the common gendered pitfall of apologizing for asking for something, what you should do is engender true connections and outreach long before you need anything. "Your asks are much more likely to be successful if they occur against the backdrop of genuine connection and kindness."

CHANNEL YOUR INNER SEINFELD

Comedians are brilliant at reading a room. You don't have to be as funny as Seinfeld, Poehler, or Thurston, however. But what comics do effectively is to read people, especially their energy and that of a crowd. It can take years to master how to thrive off the feedback of an audience. But that's precisely the model you should follow in an interview, pitch, or ask: read the room. Whether your audience is in the thousands or just one person sitting across from you having coffee: people don't want to be talked *at*. They don't want to just feel like a receptacle for your information. Even the highest stakes interview should feel like a two-way conversation. Whoever you're speaking to should be just as active a participant; they want to be involved and work *with* you. After all, comedians aren't really "performing," and you shouldn't be either. The greatest comedians—and the reason why audiences love them—are skilled at quickly engaging with the people in the audience, asking questions, listening, observing, processing, and reflecting information back to them. The audience feels seen and understood; they feel like they know the comic personally. It's the same in business: the ask is a fluid conversation.

And if someone can't give you the thing you *think* you want, how can you reframe what you get and make the most of it? The same questions apply in reverse: If someone asks you for help (which, of course, you're offering with your handshake), how can you approach the situation if you can't give them what they need? This all comes back to valuing what each of us has to offer as part of the big picture of the business of life.

BE CLEAR AND DIRECT

In addition to expecting the *yes*, I always suggest that you communicate in a way that elevates your power. This is another mistake that I see people make. In what can feel like a (false!) sense of safety or protection from the possibility of failure, it's not uncommon— especially for women—to speak in a modest or self-deprecating way. And while an ego-fueled boast or narcissistic overshare on social media won't win you any friends, your clarity, courage, and confidence will. Byng was on the Forbes 30 under 30 list for founding Her Agenda, as well as for winning an Emmy as part of a news break team at NBC New York. She was on the stage at the United State of Women Summit, hosted by the White House under the Obama administration. And when she makes an introduction or an ask, she doesn't have to hide her accomplishments. Instead, it reframes how people see a young woman of color and what she is capable of achieving. It showcases a different narrative than what is commonly presented in the media. When any woman accomplishes things— especially if they are from an underrepresented community—we must share it so the next generation can see what's possible.

All women are underrepresented when it comes to positions of power. Byng says that if you feel nervous about making an ask, you can remove yourself from the situation and place the attention back on your mission. If your objective is "to stop homelessness," then it doesn't sound so scary to ask for that person's email to see about their entry-level opportunities or to see if that person would like to contribute financially to your cause. If you are clear on your purpose—it will permeate through every ask you make, every social media post you write, and everything that you do.

In any relationship, clarity and clear communication are immensely valuable. No one can help you get what you want unless they know what that is. You can't make any expectations or assumptions that just because you sell educational software and you've been having coffee for months on end with the superintendent of the school district he will realize that you would like him to buy your software. Even if the ask seems blatantly apparent to you—you need to be crystal clear about what you want. Here are a few starter phrases that help me begin the ask by stating what I would like to achieve:

> "Here is what I need from you and your organization or company..."

> "Here is what I'm hoping to get out of this moving forward."

> "This position is great for me right now, because eventually what I'd like to do is XYZ."

And of course, if you're making genuine friendships along the way, you won't have to be so formulaic about it. It will feel right and sound right when the connection is deep.

SPEAK UP! A GUIDE
FOR INTROVERTS

It happens time and time again: I'll meet with a potential client or mentee with a home-run résumé, an ironclad project plan, or an idea that will *actually* save the world. And yet her (and usually it's "her") demeanor belies all of that brilliance. Introversion is real, and while I've always been blessed with the gift (sometimes curse) of talking and socializing, some of the most effective and powerful partners and clients I've had have been introverts. How is that possible? If you're not the kind of person to walk over to Marc Benioff and ask him for a job or tell him about your new patent—or get excited by the buzz of a 200-person cocktail party in a ballroom—you can still be an effective connector *and* have a killer career. But the tips in this section work for everyone, even if you're not introverted, since we all get uncomfortable or inwardly focused sometimes. We will also find ourselves working with introverts, so understanding what they need to thrive and support their vision, whether they're our client or our colleague, will ensure that everyone feels engaged and represented.

For years I watched in awe the skills of one of the very few female executives at PR Newswire during the 1990s, Shari Coulter Ford, whom I am still in touch with after 20 years. She would run executive team meetings filled with men and keep them all at bay and literally in fear as she would be silent for the vast majority of the time. By observing her, I learned the power that silence can have, and how if used effectively, it can keep everyone on their toes, regardless of any power discrepancy.

Silence can be a powerful strength and certainly keeps those in the room guessing what is on the person's mind.

INTROVERSION VERSUS ANXIETY

We tend to conflate social anxiety or shyness with introversion. But they are two very different things. Introversion and extroversion are defined by how you derive energy: Do you recharge best in quiet reflection? Or do you get a boost in energy from other people? An extrovert, like me, feeds off of the energy of others. Some introverts are perfectly fine being alone and don't need a lot of social stimulation, but others enjoy being around others—they just need time to recharge afterward. Social anxiety is independent of whether or not you're an introvert or an extrovert; social anxiety stems from a fear of being criticized or judged. Social anxiety can affect both introverts and extroverts. I'm an extrovert, but I also experience that fearful voice in my head at times. Being an introvert does not automatically mean that person has anxiety about being around other people. Being afraid of how others perceive us contributes to social anxiety and it can happen to any one of us.

Over and over again in my career I've seen that success and power are not limited to those with the gift of gab. In fact, those of us who do love to talk are sometimes missing what's been said, but our schools, workplaces, and cultures tend to prize talkativeness as a key to success. As Susan Cain pointed out in her book *Quiet: The Power of Introverts in a World That Can't Stop Talking*, we live in a culture that rewards extroversion and categorizes introversion "somewhere between a disappointment and a pathology." But introverts tend to be fantastic listeners, and deeply hearing what others have to say is anything but a liability in building relationships. Morra Aarons-Mele is another successful introvert. She has worked with the world's leading organizations and institutions on digital marketing campaigns since 1999, especially in the political arena. She helped Hillary Clinton log on for her first Internet chat, was the director of Internet marketing for the Democratic National Committee during the 2004 presidential election, and was BlogHer's first political director. Even though she describes herself as an introvert, Aarons-Mele is an expert on the art of connecting. She's also the author of *Hiding in the Bathroom: How to Get out There When You'd Rather Stay Home*. As she argues in her book, inwardness is a superpower, not a flaw. Aarons-Mele wrote her book because she wanted to share the methods she's developed over 20 years of building a fantastic business network in the way that works for her, a self-avowed introvert. She says the key is discerning who is most important to your career, who brings you new business and clients? Who are the people in your life who open up access to new social networks? She wrote the book as a guide for people who are extremely ambitious and want to have a great career but also want more control over the pace, place, and space of how they work and interact with others.

Instead of trying to change your disposition and seek to become what Cain calls "the extrovert ideal: the omnipresent belief that the ideal self is gregarious, alpha, and comfortable in the spotlight," Aarons-Mele tells introverts to lean into their strengths. You don't have to become the chattiest person in the room to get the most out of a gathering. (And if you want to hide in the bathroom, she says that's OK, too.)

PARTNER WITH A SUPER CONNECTOR

One of the most effective strategies for those sensitive to overstimulation: partner with a super connector. We super connectors thrive off of connecting others and love to play matchmaker. (I do think I must have been a Yenta in an earlier life.) Once you have them in your constellation, you can ask that person questions like, "Who should I talk to about getting a job in fashion?" Leverage their networks so that you can be intentional and protective about yours. In *Hiding in the*

Bathroom, Aarons-Mele calls this technique "adopting an extrovert." But I suggest taking it one step further: connect with someone who is not only an extrovert, but also a super connector. Pick someone who knows *everyone* in your field. Do you want to work in media? Find *the* super connector, the person who is ultra-plugged-into that network. Then you can leverage their networking skills in a very intentional way that won't deplete you. Preconnect with your super connector before the event to learn who you should prioritize meeting.

Lois Weisberg was one such super connector like this. In fact, she was an uber-connector—and the epitome of the "how can I help" ethos.[1] If you can meet someone like her, she would be *the* person to preconnect with! In his book *The Tipping Point*, Malcolm Gladwell described her as being a super connector within 15 to 20 different powerful communities. Weisberg was enmeshed in the lives of doctors, lawyers, financiers, actors, writers, and politicians. Weisberg lived in Chicago where she was known for her ability to meet, to connect, and to facilitate political, cultural, and economic work that would help make the city of Chicago a better place—all by being generous and sincere. When she passed away at the age of 90 in 2016, an article of remembrance in the *Chicago Tribune* was titled "The Remarkable Lois Weisberg: Famous as a Connector, but Really a Producer."

Weisberg knew what I've been saying all along about the constellation effect. Meeting and connecting is for a higher purpose—action. Yes, the purpose of these relationships is to enrich and nourish your life, but the greater intention is also to leave this world a better place than it is today. The two concepts are related, of course. If you can look back on your life as Weisberg no doubt did and feel that you not only built meaningful relationships, but also through that constellation of connections you created art, solved social problems, helped people in distress, or somehow tackled issues that the world desperately needs to solve, then the "connecting" is also about "producing" something wonderful together—and *that* is what sustains you and nurtures your soul.

SCAFFOLD YOUR EVENTS

You can also make going to professional events much easier if you give yourself a bit of scaffolding—some structure to hold the event together. So it's not just you walking into a sea of 300 people and then sprinting directly to the bathroom. To this end, I also recommend you join forces with other introverts. Touch base beforehand and compare notes on how you plan to meet people at the event but not end up drained.

Another tip? The one-third rule: You don't have to do all of the talking, or even half—aim for one-third. (And if you're the extrovert, aim to talk one-third less.) While people who tend to draw inward might find such events stressful or overwhelming, with these containers around the event, it can lessen the anxiety. Be armed with your super connector, who will meet more people than you and make introductions for you afterward. Knowing that you can listen far more than you have to talk can already make the event feel more tolerable and bearable before you get there. And hopefully, you will enjoy it more. Just be sure you don't stick to your connector like glue or you'll miss the entire point.

NAIL THE EVENT TRIUMVIRATE

Aarons-Mele also suggests setting a goal for events before you get there. I recommend what I call the event triumvirate: meet three people, learn three new ideas, share three things. (And then you can lock eyes with your fellow introvert pal and go order room service.) With that strategy, you have a clear goal and know the value you will get from the event. You can follow up with those three people and ask, Was there anyone else at the event I should talk to about breaking into journalism? Then follow up with your super connector too and ask them: What did I miss? Who should I talk to? Even if your actual appearance at the event is brief, with some thoughtful strategies, you can leverage the impact.

ORIGINALITY IS YOUR SUPERPOWER

Introverts are largely misunderstood and significantly under-valued. The world at large is set up to reward the extrovert ideal: schools, networking events, open floor plan office spaces, conferences, even Zoom or Hangout meetings during the COVID-19 pandemic—but research has shown that group conversations can bend our thoughts, opinions, and decisions toward groupthink.[2] The term *groupthink* was coined by social psychologist Irving L. Janis in 1972.[3] Groupthink is a psychological phenomenon where people in groups prioritize achieving a consensus among the group above expressing their individual opinions. In groups—whether it's at the office, at home, or while sitting on a jury—when groupthink occurs those with divergent or contrary opinions often stay quiet, preferring instead to achieve agreement. We are greatly influenced by the people we are with, even down to the level of who we find attractive. Psychologist Jamil Zaki found that if you're with a group of individuals looking at a picture of someone they find attractive, you will consider that person more attractive than you would have otherwise.[4]

To really—truly, without the influence of others—know what you think about a person, a business venture, a concept, anything really, you need time for quiet reflection. And this is a tremendous asset, so use it. Gregory Berns, an Emory University neuroscientist, found that when people take a stand that's different from that of the group, they have heightened activity in their amygdala, the part of the brain that's sensitive to rejection.[5] Berns calls this the "pain of independence." Cain says that in school and in business, you are rewarded for gregariousness and being loud. But as an introvert, you have the power of being original and pensive.

So whatever is your particular flavor of recharging your batteries, whether you're an introvert, an extrovert, an ambivert—or not really quite any of those three options—there is value in each type, and one needn't be the loudest person in the room to be a deep connector.

COMMUNICATION 101

Pings, bleeps, blurts—these sounds pepper the landscape of our days. We live in a world of nonstop communication that happens across a head-spinning number of channels, time zones, and even languages. There are myriad ways and tools (a LinkedIn note, phone call, a personal email, a quick Twitter DM) to communicate—and *mis*communicate. The challenges are many: How do you communicate in a way that is efficient but not terse? How do you make your communications authentic and deep without inadvertently crossing a professional or cultural line? How do you draw boundaries to allow for critical personal time to avoid burnout, but also make yourself flexible and available? Striking the right balance in each of these pursuits requires prioritizing openness and transparency, as well as seeing the humanity of each person—valuing the relationship above all else, including the one with yourself.

PICK UP THE PHONE

Just as we can't always meet IRL, we also can't always talk face-to-face or by phone. For that reason, digital missives are the de facto mode of communication in business. Nearly 90 percent of working professionals prefer email for their business communications.[1] If your inbox is overflowing, you're not alone. The average office worker receives 121 emails per day.[2] Add to that the Slack pings and LinkedIn messages, texts, tweets, DMs, and Teams chats, and it's no wonder burnout is on the rise. The sheer volume of our e-communications can cause myriad opportunities for misunderstandings. So yes, digital communication is key—but like connecting itself, it's an art. First consider whether a quick phone call is preferable. Is there something emotional or heated that you need to discuss? Is this particular conversation one in which you need to accurately gauge the person's reactions? Without hand gestures, facial cues, or head nodding, it can be difficult to discern what a colleague is thinking or feeling over email or Slack. When someone writes to you in an email, "I wasn't copied on that report," it is hard to know: Are they frustrated? Or offering you a friendly heads-up? Behavioral scientists have found that we make incorrect assumptions about what people mean over digital communications. We can also feel more comfortable saying something in a digital communication that we would never say face-to-face. This is called cyber-disinhibition. It's the lack of inhibition that can come from email or online communication because you don't *see* or *feel* the other person's reaction.[3] Before you write anything—an email, a text, a Slack comment—ask yourself: Is this the best channel of communication for this message? Consider, too, the volume of digital messages received in a given day. It's worth asking: Is this message even necessary? If the missive will further solidify and develop the relationship, communicate something of value, or clear up a potential misunderstanding, the answer is *yes*.

PRACTICE RELATIONALISM

When you communicate with others, regardless of the medium, keep the focus on the bigger picture. In business, it's easy to let individualism drive your communications: How will my interactions with this person affect me? How can they help me? *Me, me, me.* But viewing communication channels, styles, and messages through the lens of relationalism places the priority not on how many relationships you have, but rather on their thickness and depth. The Relationalist Manifesto, which appears at the conclusion of David Brook's book *The Second Mountain*, as well as in the Aspen Institute's project Weave: The Social Fabric Project, views communications and relationships in this way.[4] You're an individual, but you don't stand alone, you are part of a collective whole. As the business and interruptions of the workday put pressure on you to send out your emails and texts quickly, it's important to keep a relationalist framework in mind: How can you communicate with this person in a way that deepens your commitment to each other, as well as your shared goals and values? How can you pave the way for deep conversation, mutual comfort, or impactful work in a way that builds beauty and depth? Not every relationship needs to go this deep, of course, but every single human relationship you have in business—and every communication you send—should strengthen the notion that you see this person as a whole human. Resist the urge to generalize or see the person as a transaction or a spreadsheet. Our society has grown increasingly individualistic. The ego often drives our communication: What is in it for me? What's the easiest and fastest way to get this issue taken care of? But for relationships to truly be deep and meaningful, the symbiotic needs to come to the forefront.

It's better to take the approach of Weave: The Social Fabric Project, which identifies a quiet and often overlooked movement of people trying to weave the fabric of society back together, to create cohesion and common identity rather than distrust and isolation.[5] The Social Fabric Project is a program of the Aspen Institute, launched in 2018 with the idea that "social fragmentation is the central problem of our time—isolation, alienation, and division."

As David Brooks says on the Aspen Institute's website:

> The Weaver movement is repairing our country's social fabric, which is badly frayed by distrust, division and exclusion. People are quietly working across America to end loneliness and isolation and weave inclusive communities. Join us in shifting our

culture from hyper-individualism that is all about personal success, to relationalism that puts relationships at the center of our lives.

Rather than embracing an individualist perspective that places self over society, where the self is grandiose and the collective is weak—which breeds the crisis of connection many of us face—Weavers see the value in the middle ground between collective and individual. Just keeping this concept in mind as you write can be helpful: Am I writing in a way that is overtly transactional? Or am I communicating in a way that breeds *weaving*—cohesion and depth rather than deepening separateness?

Any email, text, or message you write and don't deliver face-to-face can be misconstrued. When you don't know someone's personality, as you would say with a colleague you've known for decades, it is easy to misunderstand the intention or meaning behind the words. You can easily tell when your brother is being sarcastic, but it's difficult to accurately discern sarcasm from someone else. A 2005 study in the *Journal of Personality and Social Psychology* found that we think we are better at discerning tone in email than we really are.[6] In that study, the participants *thought* they were accurately detecting whether the email sender's intent was to be serious or sarcastic, but they only judged accurately 56 percent of the time. This is about as accurate as flipping a coin to determine the result. However, the study found that when those same messages were delivered over voice, the accuracy jumped up to 73 percent. Management scholar Kristin Byron of Syracuse University says that email (or digital communication) misinterpretation typically occurs in two ways: neutral or negative.[7] We tend to interpret positive messages as neutral and neutral ones as negative. Emotions don't always come across over email, so it's helpful to use phrases like "I would be happy to" or "I am frustrated by" when communicating your feelings to colleagues.

The bottom line: for sensitive or important conversations, reach out by phone. And if you feel put off by someone else's email, take these findings into account and consider the fact that it could be a misinterpretation. Remember, you can always *ask* the recipient which format they prefer.

BE EXPLICITLY KIND

Email. Text. Slack. Zoom. Conference call. The options you have to communicate with your team, clients, or with colleagues are seemingly unlimited. But one truth remains: communicating with kindness pays off. Research on psychology, leadership, management, and neuroscience show that meaning, joy, and satisfaction can come from the very relationships and communication we build with others in our work. We don't have to suffer and slog through work email and find joyful connection only after work. In fact, joy and meaning can come *during* the workday, and not just as something we experience in the evening with our shoes kicked off. Emiliana Simon-Thomas and Dachler Keltner have been researching the concept of happiness at work at the Greater Good Science Center in Berkeley, California. What they found is that how people communicate with each other at work plays an important role in happiness, especially when it comes to kindness.[8] Simon-Thomas has been developing a set of online courses for the center called The Science of Happiness at Work.[9] Happy relationships at work not only make us more productive and effective (boosting problem solving, productivity, career advancement, creativity), but they also boost our ability to have positive relationships at work. (Which, in turn, increases our ability to be effective at our jobs, creating a positive upward spiral.) It comes as no surprise that effective communication is an important component of happy relationships. And research has shown that people who are happy in their jobs are rated by others as more likable, more trustworthy, and more deserving of respect and attention.[10] To boost happiness in your work and in your relationships Simon-Thomas came up with what she calls the PERK framework (purpose, engagement, resilience, and kindness), which can be used for effective communication.[11] Her research reveals that communicating with kindness—whether it's an email to ask how a colleague is doing, a text to say hello, or a thumbs-up Slack emoticon to denote a job well done—is good business. Even if you're reluctant to use emojis for fear of appearing unprofessional, when used sparingly in the right context—on Slack for instance—emojis can build rapport. Especially with the understanding that digital communications can be so easily misconstrued, it's worthwhile to be proactive about doling out words of kindness and gratitude.

DON'T DIMINISH YOUR E-POWER

Your email, like all communication, should be clear, kind, and succinct. It will likely land in an inbox or smartphone screen among a pile of hundreds of other messages, so be respectful of the recipient's time. But communicating with respect and kindness doesn't mean you need to put yourself last. You can—and should—uphold your power. Words are potent. Your word choice can amplify or diminish your power. You can use language that recognizes someone else's humanity but maintains your position, too.

Roneesha Byng recommends communicating in a way that is clear and kind but also powerful. At Her Agenda, she recently held a webinar with psychologist Lisa Lloyd to distill these communication tips. Avoid words that protect or soften your message in a way that is detrimental to your power. Words like *just, hoping, thinking*, or *probably* are protector words that dilute your message and your confidence. Also avoid weak language like "I'll try" or "sorry." Stating your message without these weakening words will convey your message in a more powerful way, but still leave room for connection. You also want to avoid adverbs that aren't necessary and can weaken your message: *very, absolutely* or *totally*.

To write an effective email, Byng recommends four elements: greeting, how you know them, what's in it for *them*, and a brief sign-off. Whether you're crafting an introduction email, following up after an interview, or reaching out to colleagues on your team to get a status update on a project you're working on together, this format will help you keep things professional and succinct while retaining the power that you inherently hold. The sign-off is particularly important to get right: Do you say "thanks" or "best" or "all my best?" The way you sign-off in a digital missive can also communicate (or in some instances diminish) your power. For example, I often see colleagues sign-off with "thanks" when they haven't asked the recipient for anything. Saying "thanks" without a request is like saying "thank you for reading this email," which isn't very powerful and probably not the intended message. I like to sign-off emails with "Warmly, Susan." It's friendly, it's professional, and it doesn't take away power.

And then, of course, there's the question we should all be asking before we send an email at all: Do I *need* to send this email? Would a quick phone call or Slack message be better? Simplicity and brevity are key—as with all forms of communication and connection, use your email judiciously.

DMS FOR DEEP AND AUTHENTIC CONNECTION

Social media has a lot of negative rap when it comes to creating meaningful relationships—or even being a good use of time. But a direct message over Instagram, Facebook, LinkdedIn, or any social media platform *can* forge a deep connection when used appropriately. In fact, when she was incredibly sick with COVID-19, CNN journalist and anchor Brooke Baldwin said that the DMs she received on Instagram were what carried her through. In the spring 2020, as she was reporting on the coronavirus pandemic, suddenly Baldwin became so ill that she could not do her job. She lost her sense of taste and smell, became so fatigued that she could hardly stand, and was so terrified and overwhelmed by how sick she was that at night—sleeping apart from her husband to protect his health—she would weep. But in the early days of her illness, when she was able to, she shared her experiences on Instagram—and the messages of support she received were a lifeline.

In Baldwin's words:

It was as simple as commenting on an Instagram post or sending me a DM. When I was up for it, I would start chipping away at my messages and respond. I heard from people who were grateful for the inspiration and that I didn't sugar-coat it. I heard from people who lost loved ones to COVID and wanted to just tell me their story. I heard from so many people who have just felt afraid and lonely. And we connected—digitally.

Most memorable—FaceTiming with my mom. She holds her iPad on her lap which meant I saw up her nose a lot more than I needed—but hey my septuagenarian mother was getting hip with her iPhone and wanted to check on me A LOT—and I let her.

And then once I had finally made the turn and was feeling more like myself—I jumped on a Zoom with my three closest girlfriends and it nearly brought tears to my eyes.

When you view someone as a whole human and not merely a data point, a transaction, or a vehicle to a close a sale, these kinds of genuine connections can transpire. What also allowed Baldwin to experience that level of connection with friends and colleagues alike was her vulnerability, by sharing her harrowing experience with the illness. She opened herself up and demonstrated that she was not only a broadcast journalist, but also a human being who gets sick, grieves, feels fear, and needs human connection to survive and thrive. When you communicate in a way that humanizes that person, that sees them as a daughter, a friend, someone who experiences grief, loss, fear, triumph, and joy, the particular medium isn't important.

On the flip side, digital relationships can create a false sense of intimacy. If we follow someone online, we may *think* we know someone, but all we really know is what's public about them: images shared on social media, media mentions, a LinkedIn CV, data points like where they grew up or went to college. And while this can be useful when establishing an initial connection, it can lead us astray if we allow it to paint a picture of the whole person. Stacy London, the stylist, author, magazine editor, and cohost of *What Not to Wear*, says that the very reason we can misfire and misconnect digitally can be due to technology itself. As London points out, you can't rush discovery process of getting to know someone IRL—the blossoming of a relationship. If you do rush that process, it can create that false sense of intimacy and connection. Relationships take time and we can use technology to supplement what we glean from each other face-to-face, but it cannot speed up intimacy and real connection.

But as long as you're being "authentic," true connection can transpire, right? According to Herminia Ibarra, professor of organizational behavior at London Business School, maybe not. *Authenticity* has become a bit of a buzzword, but what does authenticity even mean? Ibarra is one of the most influential management thinkers in the world. Her TED Talk, the "Authenticity Paradox," as well as a thought-provoking article in *Harvard Business Review* by the same name, points out the surprising notion that even the term *authenticity* itself can be a crutch.[12] She argues that when we too narrowly or rigidly define what our "authentic self" is and what it stands for, it can serve as an excuse for staying in our comfort zone. With an overly simplistic view of who we are, it can limit our impact, and I would argue, our ability to connect with others outside of our comfort zone. Ibarra argues that we learn the most when our sense of self is challenged. But when we see ourselves as a work in progress, and our identities as constantly evolving, we can be both authentic and in a position to learn and grow out of our comfort zone by putting ourselves in conversations and engaging in communications that may be uncomfortable. Authentic doesn't always mean comfortable—and that's exactly the point.

In Baldwin's case, she used social media as way to chronicle her illness, and as a result, it became a channel of connection for her, a link to the outside world, with whom she couldn't connect face-to-face while ill. She said that it was challenging for her to be the center of attention like that, but it was transformative and powerful, too, having a lasting effect on how she will communicate going forward. Baldwin says that when she was sick, she turned often to the words of Brené Brown, who could be called the godmother of vulnerability. Baldwin especially found comfort in this particular quote from Brown's work: "Staying vulnerable is a risk we have to take if we want to experience connection."

GIVE FEEDBACK WHEN NEEDED

Clear, effective, and authentic communication also includes feedback, a critical component of healthy business relationships. It's a step in the relationship that requires vulnerability: telling someone what you don't like about something they've said, done, or created. But when you learn how to skillfully say hard things well, feelings of closeness, connection, and respect can transpire. Think about it: Has anyone ever given you some feedback—perhaps told you something you didn't necessarily want to hear—but you ended up having more respect for them because you know it took courage to say? Especially when it's delivered with skill and with kindness, giving feedback can be—somewhat counterintuitively—a gateway to greater intimacy. In her book *Mastering Civility*, Christine Porath, a professor of Business at Georgetown University's McDonough School of Business, relays how small acts of respect can add up over time, building not only your credibility but also the bottom line.[13] Giving people news that needs to be shared, when done respectfully, can build upon existing respect. And feedback should never be given in a way that is rude. Porath points out how rudeness in the workplace is not only destructive to relationships, but also hurts productivity and efficiency, too. In short, drama and incivility between coworkers costs us all, so it pays to give feedback in a way that builds rather than tears down a relationship. And when you do, you may find an unexpected result: appreciation.

If you need to give someone feedback, do so in a way that strengthens the relationship. Fran Hauser recommends communicating in a way that is both kind and direct. Hauser says that when you communicate kindly, it will allow the recipient to hear you and doing so directly will ensure they understand the feedback that you are giving them. Stacy London recommends lending your constructive criticism with an eye toward *creation*, to literally create something new. London says that if she is doing her job effectively, she is helping someone else to envision and create the life that *they* want—not the one that she wants. Maybe it's helping them view a blind spot, showing them something that they cannot see. And that's the goal of effective feedback: giving someone some information that will ultimately help *them*, not you. This is a good barometer for whether your feedback is friendly or rude: Are your statements serving to make *you* feel better (most likely, in the moment), or are you delivering it in a way that will help the recipient be a better colleague, mentor, or interviewee?

When you're able to deliver feedback skillfully in this way, the recipient should feel as though they are receiving a pep talk or some inside scoop that will help them grow from a friend. This is what Daisy Auger-Dominguez refers to as the practice of *calling in* versus calling out. Calling in is a practice of bringing someone *in* to have a conversation about something you want to bring to their attention, rather than saying "hey, you did this wrong" and making a call out in a punitive way. Auger-Dominguez has spent her entire impressive career expertly navigating cultural and racial identity in the workplace. A Dominican–Puerto Rican–New Yorker, Auger-Dominguez has spent the last 20 years designing and implementing diversity, equity, and inclusion strategies for companies such as Google, Walt Disney Company, Moody's, and now VICE Media. Auger-Dominguez says that we live in a cancel culture where if you don't like what someone has to say, you can just cancel them out. But instead, she suggests reaching out with the spirit of building connection to say, "Hey, you did this hurtful thing, but I'm not going to punish you, I want to bring it to your attention."

Auger-Dominguez says the goal is for reconciliation, not retribution. When you deliver feedback to someone in this way, you can say anything you want and it will be interpreted in a way that will build, rather than tear apart, the rapport.

BE MINDFUL OF OTHERING AND BIAS

Even if you're doing everything you can to be authentic, connect with kindness, and see the whole person, miscommunication will still happen. The reality is, we all have biases; some are hidden and pernicious. Nine out of ten people say that America is more divided than it's ever been at any point in their lifetime.[14] We live in isolated information bubbles and can even draw wildly different conclusions from the same set of raw data. Our perceptions—of others, of data, of ourselves—are often misguided. We need to all remain aware of our unconscious bias as much as we possibly can and to admit fault when necessary, to make repairs when appropriate, and to embrace discomfort and do the important work to rid ourselves of such biases. Dr. Jennifer Eberhardt is a social psychologist at Stanford University. In her book, *Biased: Uncovering the Hidden Prejudice That Shapes What We See, Think, and Do,* she writes, "At its root, bias is not an affliction that can be cured or banished; it's a human condition that we have to understand and deal with." There is some evidence that becoming aware of bias can help reduce it.[15] Research suggests that recognizing that human traits are more malleable than fixed—that how people behave is somewhat dependent on environmental circumstances—decreases stereotyping.[16] And a long line of research shows that increasing positive intergroup interactions where personal relationships can develop between people of different social groups can decrease bias, too, as long as the people involved are of equal status and of good will.[17]

The Hidden Tribes of America is a yearlong project launched by More in Common in late 2018 to examine the forces that catalyze political polarization and separation in the United States today, to understand what causes tribalism, and to spearhead efforts to address these issues.[18] According to the Hidden Tribes report, though we think we are divided across lines of race, geography, education, class, and values, this report argues that we are less divided than we think.[19] What we suffer from most is a *perception gap*, and an important driver of this gap is the fact that the voices on the extreme ends of each view or argument are the loudest and do not necessarily represent the majority. It's important not to let algorithms and the perception gap deepen our disconnection. Rather, when we can see each other as humans and not make assumptions based on our job or tweet, when we seek to get to know the other person and not assume that we know them based on what they did or didn't do, then we can bridge these divides and genuine communication can result. This doesn't mean we compromise our values, but instead, as the report recommends, we should prioritize "understanding over judgment, openness over dogma, and empathy over exclusion."

When it comes to digital communication, it's important to note what "language" does this person speak? Taking the time and effort to learn the terms they use (for example, if they work in philanthropy, do they prefer the term *donation* and not *gift*?) will communicate effort and respect. Any efforts you can make to speak the *language* of the person you're communicating with will reap significant rewards. And of course, this takes time and effort, which is why it is so effective.

John A. Powell and Stephen Menendian argue that the main problem we face in the twenty-first century is that of "othering."[20] The idea is that human beings have a tendency to put themselves and others in social categories, and to judge members of their own category as superior to that of the other. Placing anyone—a colleague, a business associate, any human being—in the category of an "other" breeds distrust, loneliness, inequality, and alienation. This innate habit of othering, of using "we versus them" thinking can breed disconnection, too.

Ruth Ann Harnisch, the investor, activist, philanthropist, former news anchor, and radio talk-show host, says that rather than throwing people into categories, we should view each relationship as its own unique entity—a design as unique as a fingerprint. Harnisch says that human beings love generalizations, rules, and categories—but when it comes to human generalizations, the only rule is that there are none. Individuals are completely unique in the way they ascribe meaning as well as the way they communicate. To address that, you should constantly ask for clarification. Asking for the right time to have hard conversations helps too. "When would be a good time to talk to you about this issue?" This question takes the pressure off the other person. They are not forced to have a hard conversation they aren't prepared for. You're letting them know that you would like to talk about hard things, but you are giving them control around *when that happens*. You can also use this technique to deepen the relationship: "Are you interested in a meaningful relationship with me? What would that look like for you?"

DRAW BOUNDARIES AND USE SELF-CARE TO AVOID BURNOUT

According to the World Health Organization, burnout is a state of mental distance, feelings of negativism and cynicism related to one's job.[21] Ironically, being constantly "on" and digitally connected to others can lead to burnout, which exacerbates feelings of isolation, disconnection, and loneliness. If you feel overwhelmed and exhausted, this is a signal to take care of yourself and draw some boundaries. Doing so will make you more productive, and happier, too. Social psychologists, organizational behavioralists, and human resource professionals say that job-related burnout is on the rise. Two-thirds of working professionals say they have experienced burnout.[22] When it is possible, if not preferable, to be constantly on, it's paramount that you be intentional and vigilant about your time "off."

Harnisch says that ultimately the most trusted relationship you need to build is with yourself. She recommends becoming your own most trusted connection of all. Harnisch tracks the pro bono hours that she offers each month and then says no to the rest of requests she receives. If you make an agreement with yourself—stick to it. If you tell yourself that you will stay offline on Sundays, follow through. If this is a challenge for you, start small and build from there. Build trust with yourself that you will follow through, just like you would with a stranger. Harnisch recommends starting with an achievable commitment so that you can't fail, and over time you will become a person who never fails to keep their commitments to themselves.

WHEN IN DOUBT, OVERCOMMUNICATE

When relationships thrive, it almost always happens because the two people in the relationship are both good at listening as well as sharing information and feelings. If you think about most failed business relationships, deals, or partnerships, one of the common denominators is a disparity between expectations and reality. In other words: a miscommunication. You thought you were getting one thing, but actually received another. So compensating for that by overcommunicating, especially now, is a great way to avoid the communication wires getting crossed, or worse—breaking. Laurie Segall is an American journalist known for interviewing leaders in technology such as Mark Zuckerberg and Tim Cook. She was the senior technology correspondent and an editor-at-large for CNN for more than a decade. According to Segall, who now runs Dot Dot Dot, a news and entertainment company exploring the intersection of tech and humanity, "The secret weapon to building a meaning-ful connection in a business sense is finding a human connection." And Segall and others I spoke to for this book point out that it is critical to overcommunicate, as the human tendency tends to be to undercommunicate. Segall points out that online communication just doesn't provide a clear means of communication, as we weren't fit to experience humanity through the lens of a screen. What hap-pens is that context—over Zoom, text, or email—gets lost. So it's incredibly important to overcommunicate—use emojis to state how you feel about what you are saying, and reiterate what you mean even if it seems obvious. Better to over- than undercommunicate. Segall also points out how digital communication doesn't breed room for serendipity and for joy. For instance, if you're in an online meeting, you don't have the ability to turn to a colleague and have a side conversation, which might lead to a creative conversation about another topic or project.

Segall also says that she worries about workplace dynamics where women may not speak up as loudly as men—or perhaps where they may not be as aggressive—and how that can translate over the screen. She says, "I think that the people coding these experiences largely are men. So we've got to start paying attention to the ethics of how people connect and communicate digitally."

When I asked her how she recommends overcommunicating, she said:

> Sometimes I leave people voice memos now. I'm trying to beta test anything that might code back humanity. So many different topics about what it means to be human have the potential to be completely disrupted in a post pandemic world. I think technology is going to play such an extraordinary role in that, and I'm looking forward to shaping stories with nuance and with care, and to examine it through an ethical lens.

Segall is doing exactly that at Dot Dot Dot. The company aims to examine how technology impacts human beings as well as what the human relationship is with technology itself. Segall points out that the way human beings have conversations right now using technology is broken—and that there is such a huge opportunity for innovation and positive change in this space. As she was reporting on technology and watching it become such an integral part of everyday human life, she saw a gaping hole. For instance Segall's company is currently working on developing something called haptic technology. "Haptic technology," Segall explains, " was already kind of something people were talking about, but now it's technology to replace human touch."

Now this can be a total game changer to how we connect and communicate in the future. As I've said all throughout this book, technology can be the cure or it can be the disease itself—it's all in the dosage that we use and how we use it. Are we using it to add depth and connection, or are we leaning on it as a tool to stay iso-lated? It's about how we, as humans who love that dopamine hit, can resist the urge to use our tools in ways that hurt our human connections.

Segall also said that as she navigated CNN, advancing from a news assistant to the senior technology correspondent, much of her success happened with little emails and funny conversations and in a sense, overcommunicating with the people she worked with, whether it was being overly clear when an issue came up, or spend-ing her free time talking to other editors to get to know them better and learn from them. Segall says that she used to go to the back into the control rooms where the cameras recorded guests, and just talk to the team members who worked there. She also used to spend her free time sitting with one of the editors at CNN to watch him do his craft—edit. And as she puts it, "It was those human conversations I had and the context of business that really made a difference."

ASK REVIEW: WHAT WE'VE LEARNED

In this second part of the book, *Ask*, we've covered how to move into the next phase of establishing deeper, more meaningful rela-tionships. While in part one, *Gather*, we reviewed all of the different creative and proactive ways I suggest for bringing a broad and impactful set of people into your world, in the *Ask* chapters, I hope you gained a sense of how to take a relationship from a casual or one-off acquaintance into a deeper and more meaningful relation-ship—one that can last a lifetime.

The first way that I suggest you do that is by asking my favorite question, "How can I help?" This changes the dynamic immediately. It alters your view and fuels learning, too. This approach can dis-solve the fear of failure, too, as when you're helping others, it's less about "success" or what you "get" and instead points you toward the expertise or experience you have to offer. Just remember, offering to help isn't about pleasing, and I encourage you to do so in ways that energize you.

When I think of the *Ask* part of my constellation approach, it's really also about getting to know this person who may become a meaningful part of your life. Listen to them, take in their advice and what they say, follow up on their advice and what they recommend, and close the loop with them, building trust and transparency. When you find yourself at events or gatherings where there are a lot of people, or perhaps you're more introverted—use the strategies we learned like finding super connectors or scaffolding the event. Give yourself some structure by going with a sidekick (your super connector would be a good one!), or walk in with a goal like what I call the event triumvirate: meet three people, learn three ideas, share three things.

Finally, whether you're asking for a job or asking if you can get to know someone else better, consider their perspective and make it easy for them. You can make it easy for someone else to say yes with tactics like the five-minute ask or offering three ways someone else can help you. And finally, when you're deepening connections in your life, pick up the darned phone. Be extra kind to people. When in doubt, overcommunicate and ask for clarity. And yes, in a pinch, even social media can be a way to deepen a relationship. When done genuinely, even a quick DM on Instagram—Are you OK? Is there anything I can do?—can work.

PART III

DO

FOCUS: Turn your connections into meaningful action. Shine a light on the causes that inspire you and make your business about more than profit and the bottom line. You made new contacts at events, through your volunteer work, through the gatherings you've hosted yourself, and even all the Zoom happy hours you joined. Now what? How do you take those connections from the realm of an acquaintance into a connection that is meaningful and deep? Through several small actions that build up over time.

THE ART OF THE
FOLLOW-UP

The goal in any meaningful relationship is to give it depth. That's what this book is all about. Of course, not every relationship you have has to go deep: we have a finite amount of time, energy, and resources. Yet for any relationship where there are potential synergies to help each other in business and in life, it's worthwhile to take the relationship deeper. And what people so often ask me is: How? How do you *do* that? How do you deepen a business relationship without feeling awkward or stiff? How do you transform a relationship from the superficial to the meaningful?

Relationships are a social, emotional, and material investment. You have to be selective about where to dedicate your energy to avoid burning out and to make certain that your energy goes where it is best directed. But there are some simple tricks and strategies that you can use to make "following up" more dynamic, less rote, and not so much of a chore. (Cue the dreaded "just wanted to follow up!" email.) Your goal with the follow-ups that you send and other actions items that you execute are to transform the connection from a "contact" (a business card, a LinkedIn profile, a Twitter account that you skim) to an actual relationship—a deeper tie, a meaningful connection. But what takes a relationship from that first handshake, fist bump, or hello to a genuine, decades-long connection? Many small, but meaningful actions in between. Here are a few.

SEW THE FIRST LINE OF CONNECTING THREAD

Let's say, for example, that you meet someone at a dinner event who works in criminal justice reform. And let's also say that you are a public relations consultant, which at first glance might have nothing to do with the nation's prison systems. It would be easy to think, "Well, that was an interesting person, but I don't see how our lines of work can intersect." I see people make this mistake all of the time. They meet someone new and when the connection and collaboration aren't immediately obvious, they miss the opportunity for a deeper connection and relationship. I see many people make the error of being shortsighted in their views of what a relationship could ultimately offer. Don't dismiss these new connections. When you first meet someone—especially if it's someone you feel a connection with or a shared passion or goal in business—you want to act right away once the doorway to the relationship has been opened to deepen that connection. What did you talk about? Is there a passion you share? Does this person have knowledge about a topic you would like to learn more about? Make that first follow-up immediately a way to solidify the connection. You want that person to have a way to remember you beyond "Oh yeah, we met at that dinner." Here are a few examples of follow-up emails I like to send:

EXAMPLE 1

It was wonderful to meet you. I'm fascinated by the work you're doing in _____ field. Please keep me posted on your work. I'd love to find ways to support you and your endeavors.

EXAMPLE 2

It was great to meet you last evening at the _____ event! Let's keep in touch. *(It really is that simple to follow up!)*

EXAMPLE 3
So great to meet you! I'd love to get to know you better and see how I might be able to support your good work. Want to grab coffee in the next several weeks?

EXAMPLE 4
I saw this article on _____ and thought of you—it was great to connect! Let's keep in touch.

As a daily practice, I send emails like the preceding ones to "thread the connection" among the people I meet in my life. I have a daily practice of sending Tweets, LinkedIn likes, text messages, phone calls, and even snail mail, to let people in my world know that I am thinking about them—that I am interested in staying connected on a deep, human level. It's like a daily watering of the garden, tending the soil. Following up not only means moving business forward, but it also means checking in on the people who are important to my business and also to my life as a whole.

TAKE ACTION RIGHT AFTER YOU MEET

You had a great meeting, a phone call, video chat, or email exchange; you delivered your presentation or managed your job interview perfectly. You have some degree of confirmation that things are moving forward. Don't stop the train midtrack! Taking follow-up action is not only essential for deepening that initial connection, but also for turning a job or idea into reality. This is another one of the biggest mistakes I see people make: they fail to follow up quickly and effectively. Using the many modes of communication we have available today, and your ever-sharpening skills of knowing what works best with which people—take immediate action steps post-meeting. Popular online articles directed at job seekers will recommend a two-week wait before sending a follow-up email post-interview. But I disagree and in fact, this immediate action can set you apart from other candidates. Instead, I recommend you demonstrate to your potential employers, clients, and partners that you're not only serious, but enthusiastic on the spot by drafting an email immediately after you meet. Connect with and follow up on their preferred social platforms, or set a reminder on your phone to take action in another way. Don't wait for the other person to take the lead. Everyone's inundated by email these days, and our attention spans are getting smaller. Close the gap and ensure your proposal or job application moves out of the digital ether.

EVERYONE WANTS TO FEEL SEEN

During each meeting that you have, jot down notes about what is important to this particular person. Are they looking to hire someone skilled in social media? Do they mention a hobby or interest that you share? Are they traveling to London this fall? Did they suggest that you listen to Rebecca Jarvis's podcast? Write all of these things down so that when you follow up, you can do so on a particular item that will prove how closely you were listening and paying attention. You can email them to say, "How was that trip to London? Did you happen to grab a lunch at Borough Market?" When you do this, the person will feel remembered and heard. As discussed earlier, what makes a relationship meaningful is when each person feels *seen*. And when you pay attention to the particulars about what's important in their work and in their life, this can be achieved easily and effortlessly.

Celebrate their wins. Is someone having a birthday? Reach out. Did they just change jobs and announce it on LinkedIn? Congratulate them. Did they or their company receive a media mention? Send them a note to let them know you saw it. You can take this practice even further by facilitating it for other people. As one example, I once hosted a book launch celebration for my friends Pavia Rosati and Jeralyn Gerber, who wrote *How to Not Be a Tourist*. The book was about how to travel all around the world and see the cities and sights as a local, not as a tourist. Rather than letting everyone introduce themselves in the usual way—"Hi, I'm Susan and I live in Brooklyn Heights,"—I had each person share one place they wanted to visit in the world. Somebody said, "Oh, I want to go to Alaska." Someone else said, "Oh I was just there." As everyone spoke, I took notes on the conversations that ensued. The next day, I sent everyone an email to thank them for coming and to once again celebrate the release of the book.

Then I added the following:

> I wrote down each person's "ideal places to visit" so each of you could reconnect and follow up with that. I hope you all find a way to travel to the place you had in mind, and now, with this new book and the new connections you made at the event, you will have a way to visit that place like a local—enjoy!

People followed up with each other and took their conversations away from the event and into the personal sphere, sharing things like travel itineraries, insights on the best place to eat in Milan, where to stay in Vancouver, or how to visit Japan with young children. What could have been a onetime, isolated event at my home was transformed into deeper connections in some cases. It didn't take me long at all, and everyone felt seen, understood, and grateful.

If you keep your mind open—and don't let your connections be limited by the people who could "do something for your business"— there are a million different insights, learnings, and opportunities for connections. Maybe someone you just met at a barbecue will someday be at the very company you wish to work for. Perhaps your father has Alzheimer's and the person you just met could lead you to the best medical care. Maybe your daughter is applying to schools and this person sits on the board of *the* school she wants to attend. Perhaps this individual you just met is championing a social or political cause that you want to get behind. The opportunities are unlimited once you change your lens of perception and start to view business relationships in this way.

FEELING SAFE AND SECURE
IS IMPORTANT, TOO

Dr. David Rock is the director of the NeuroLeadership Institute, a global initiative bringing neuroscientists and leadership experts together to build a new science for leadership development.[1] Dr. Rock and his team study the brain, and he has coined a term called *neuroleadership*, which is essentially using brain science to instruct effective leadership. Of course, for leaders, building relationships with colleagues and team members is perhaps the most important skill. What Dr. Rock and his team have discovered essentially backs up what I've been saying about the importance of making people feel *seen*. In any relationship, human beings need to feel safe, seen, and secure to take the risk of being vulnerable—of sharing their humanity, their flaws. Their *realness*. In any relationship that is going to have depth and meaning, this is essential. In his research, Dr. Rock found more detail about what that looks like in business relationships, as it relates to the human brain. As human beings, we are wired to avoid threats (*run from the tiger!*) and to accept rewards (*sugar, yum!*). And as we now know, social experiences can also create an experience of threat (getting left out of an invite, bullying) as well as a reward (receiving an invite, getting a compliment). To break this down a bit further, Dr. Rock and his team developed what's known as the SCARF model of social threat and reward, with SCARF being an acronym for the five different domains of human social experience.[2] In this model, the domains are status, certainty, autonomy, relatedness, and fairness.[3] And research has shown that these domains tend to activate the same reward circuitry in the brain as a physical reward, like money, or a physical threat, like pain. Looking at Dr. Rock's model, I noticed how the themes of feeling seen, safe and secure emerge. **Status** is a human's relative importance to others (feeling *seen*). **Certainty** is a human's desire to predict future (feeling *safe, secure*). **Autonomy** is the human sense of having control over events (feeling *safe, secure*). **Relatedness** is the human sense of relative safety with others (feeling *seen, safe*).

Fairness is the human perception of fair exchanges with others (*seen, safe*).

What Dr. Rock and his team found is that some people tend to prioritize some of these domains more than others. And if you, like me, tend to pick up on people's relational needs organically, you don't need to be overly analytical about it. You just may have a sense: this person likes to feel safe; they like to have certainty about what's coming up. But what's interesting is that Dr. Rock's research all points back to those main overarching themes of the human desire to feel *safe*, *seen*, and *secure* in our relationships with each other. And by examining Dr. Rock's model, we can pick up some actionable tips for deepening relationships or even just getting along better with our colleagues. It's also interesting to look at the model from the perspective of your own social needs: Do you tend to need status, certainty, autonomy, relatedness, or fairness most in your relationships? This paradigm can also be a useful toolkit for troubleshooting if a relationship has begun to feel rocky. Did a friend or colleague get offended at something you said or did? The SCARF model points to a clue as to why and may give you some ideas about how to reconnect: is there a way you can offer a sense of safety or security in the relationship that might retighten the connection? Dr. Rock's work makes the assumption that our brains are wired to behave in social interactions in a way that maximizes pleasure and minimizes pain. And understanding that, it offers us some scaffolding we can use to *build* a meaningful connection, by creating empathy and psychological safety.

DO THE THING THEY TOLD YOU TO DO

Telling someone you'll do something (and then taking action) is one way for you to demonstrate your trustworthiness as well as a means for helping that person feel seen. But what's less often recognized is the importance of taking action on advice or tips that other people suggest *to you*. It takes only a few minutes of your time. If a new connection suggests you order the hummus at the restaurant down the street from your apartment—try it. Then you have the perfect opportunity to reconnect with them over email. "Loved the hummus—great call!" Sending that quick email can transform that relationship from one of emotional distance into one of closeness. Did you meet someone new who suggested a book you should read? Pick it up from your local library or the bookstore—and then write them to say you did so and to thank them for the tip. Did the person mention that they were just on a podcast? Listen to the episode and send a brief note or better yet, promote the podcast on Instagram or Twitter. Not only will these actions provide context into their work and their personality, you will also have another reason to connect. After you listen to the podcast you can write: "Fascinating podcast about impact direct-to-consumer marketing—I have some friends in this space I'd love to connect you to, if you'd like?" And just like that, you're starting to further weave the connection. Or if you chose to promote on social platforms, most likely your contact will see and reap the benefits.

As you build contacts and relationships, people will give you advice. You will get myriad unsolicited tips, suggestions, and recommendations. In many cases, these tips fall on deaf ears. But as much as you can, especially in a relationship that you would like to find meaningful, you should heed the advice that you get. In fact, there's research showing that if you *don't* follow the advice a colleague or a contact gives you, it can have negative consequences. We ignore people's advice all of the time. But it pays to know that when we do, there can be negative ramifications. Don't ask a colleague or a new connection for their advice or tips (no matter how trivial) if you don't plan on taking it. Doing so is another great way to deepen a connection and to make someone feel seen. A paper published by the Harvard School of Business revealed the results of nine studies, which showed that when business leaders have their advice requested—and then not taken—it damages the relationship.[4] In these studies, the advisors whose counsel wasn't acted on, not only distanced them from their colleagues, but in some cases, they later disparaged them and even ended the relationship. Following someone else's suggestion—and then circling back with them to let them know—is a great way to deepen your tie, connection and instill trust.

MOVE THE RELATIONSHIP FORWARD

While my parents tended to their relationships by sending manually typed "I'm thinking of you" notes via the mail; today, the notes we send have the asset of instant contact via technology. I like to use my morning coffee time to send off these daily missives. I write in my email groups, share and like posts on socials, and skim the news for topics of interest or to discern where I can be of help. In what's become a cherished morning routine (while throwing a toy with my pup), I participate in a mutual exchange of support that has kept my business—and sanity—thriving. When we are in communities that keep us accountable and make us feel seen, heard, and appreciated for our contributions—no matter how big or small—we are more empowered and energized to keep on giving, making, and doing what we love.

Whether it's in the morning over coffee as I do it or at night after dinner, I encourage you to find a daily practice of following up on the meaningful people in your life. And as it turns out, *what* you discuss is as important as *how* you do it. What makes people close? What drives intimacy in any relationship? Studies show that if you're engaged in less small talk, you're happier—that's because the talk that makes us feel a connection and spark a deeper relationship isn't talk about the weather.[5] Communication is not only a skill in how you speak, listen, tweet, or write as you follow up, but it's also a skill to know *what* you should talk about. Research on the kinds of daily talk that human beings engage in (whether it's on Twitter or via your smartphone) show that there are five different types of "talk." According to a study published in the journal *Communication Theory*, there are five different layers of talk: impersonal communication, small talk and catching up, laughing and joking around, gossip, meaningful talk, self-disclosure, and affection.[6] As you might suspect, the reward—in terms of the depth of your relationship—is lowest with impersonal communication and highest with affection. But guess which kinds of talk we engage in most frequently? Yep—small talk. Or impersonal talk.

The talk that we do most frequently (*How was your weekend? Great.*) provides the least amount of value in our relationships. The reason? Self-disclosure and affection require *vulnerability*, something many of us try to avoid. Simply understanding these different types of communication, and the impact each one has on the depth and quality of your relationship, can impact the way you relate to people. You want to move further along to the more meaningful types of communication, as appropriate.

As you go through your daily routines of following up with the people in your life, make sure you're intentionally carving out ways to talk about something that is personally meaningful—this will increase your sense of closeness and related belonging. Be strategic though; you have limited resources and there is a cost to maintaining each social relationship. Not all social activity—including the notes, emails, texts, and other follow-up we do—satisfies our need to belong or strengthens relationships. I suggest you do this even in a job interview or in a brand new connection. If you can—without it feeling awkward or too much of a stretch—find a way to talk about something meaningful or personal with a potential employer, that person will likely feel a sense of indebtedness to you, a feeling of kinship. And he or she will be more likely to work with or hire you, as a result.

There are some environments where deep connection happens naturally. I try to immerse myself into as many of these communities as possible, and I highly recommend you do the same. From Meetups to conferences to WhatsApp chat groups, some gatherings are literally designed to instill a feeling of connection. One such gathering is Spark Camp, which I have been lucky enough to attend on a few occasions. *Fast Company* called it "the ultimate summer camp for influencers."[7] The brainchild of tech and media veterans Amy Webb (CEO of Future Today Institute), Amanda Michel

(*Guardian*), Matt Thompson (Center for Investigative Reporting), Andrew Pergam (Facebook), and Jennifer 8. Lee (formerly of the *New York Times*), Spark brings together talented people to tackle the world's most pressing problems and questions and to develop meaningful relationships that will inspire much-needed action. At Spark Camp, the entire weekend is carefully choreographed with deep intentionality to bring about genuine connection. A typical Spark Camp might include entrepreneurs, venture capitalists, media producers, academics, writers, and policy leaders and journalists, with a sprinkling of art curators, chefs, and musicians. Amanda Michel described it to me like this:

> At Spark Camp, people come from a place of humility, where all of the barriers have been knocked down. It's never "Oh, she's the CEO, I can't talk to her." Everyone is on a first-name basis and everyone is approachable. When those walls, barriers and biases, break down and then participants can truly just talk about what they can create together—that is when magic happens.

But even if you're not at a formal event like Spark Camp that is designed intentionally to create such an experience, you can create your own mini version of this event. Or you can simply choose to pepper your conversations, preferably in person, with the kinds of questions that weave a deep relationship. Essentially, you are extending your practice of making another person feel seen. Of asking them, in many different ways, how you can help. Though these conversations are often best executed face-to-face, when necessary video chat, phone conversation, and email can be tools to deepen the way in which to follow up.

The important skill to hone here is to have conversations that are not transactional or based on small talk or the business at hand. To that end, I have developed a set of questions to use as a jumping-off point to deepen your feelings of closeness with others. And while there is some finesse to delivering these questions (you certainly don't want to randomly fire them off in a list!), just becoming familiar with them can help broaden your sense of how to share deeper conversations with others. You can even use a few of them in a job interview or at a career networking event. Used skillfully, they can really be applied to anyone, anywhere! Many of the following questions are adapted from the *New York Times* list "36 Questions for Increasing Closeness."[89] And while *that* particular set of questions is known for causing people to fall in love, that is not the goal here! The objective in this case is to deepen a professional relationship:

1. If you could invite anyone in the world as your dinner guest, who would it be?
2. Tell me the story of your whole career in three minutes.
3. If you could change anything about the way your career has evolved, what would it be and why?
4. If you could wake up tomorrow and acquire one new professional quality or ability, what would it be? What about personal qualities?
5. Is there something you've dreamed of doing for a long time but haven't? Why haven't you done it?
6. What do you value most in a friendship?
7. If you and I were to have a more meaningful relationship with each other, what would be important for me to know?
8. I'd like to share what I admire about you: _____. What is something that you admire about me?
9. What, if anything, is too serious to be joked about?
10. Share a problem that you've been struggling with, and ask that person's advice on how he or she might handle it.

CREATE A RITUAL

Coffee on Tuesdays. A Peloton ride on Saturday. Team check-ins on Wednesdays. Rituals are powerful for creating meaning and depth. Participating in them with business colleagues is no exception. You don't need to schmooze, but to have authentic relationships, you *do* need to get to know people in a personal way. Especially if you've joined a new team, started a new role in your company, or found yourself in the position of being new on the scene in any way—it will pay to be proactive in setting up routines with your colleagues. You don't have to be disingenuous about it. In fact, you shouldn't. Ask someone to have a regular monthly coffee with you, virtually or in person. Pay attention to what they are doing in business and offer advice or connections on a regular basis, as often as you can. Think of these as opportunities to be in sync with your colleagues. Will it really make you closer? Trust me, it will. In 2014, *Harvard Business Review* reported on a study that measured the impact of participants tapping along in time to the sound of music—with other participants they didn't know.[10] The results were striking: those who tapped along to the same beat and rhythm were three times more likely to rush to the aid of their partner, as compared to those who tapped to asynchronous rhythms. Whether it's a team, a colleague, or a potential partner, shared rituals can be incredibly powerful, a way to build shared trust.

Author of the bestselling book *Bring Your Human to Work: 10 Surefire Ways to Design a Workplace That's Good for People, Great for Business, and Just Might Change the World*, Erica Keswin is a workplace strategist who has spent the last 20 years working with some of the world's most iconic brands. In her second book, *Rituals Roadmap: The New Way to Transform Everyday Routines into Workplace Magic*, she talks about how to build meaningful habits and rituals into your workday. Keswin says, "Rituals are significant because they offer us the three Ps: psychological safety, purpose, and performance." And I would add that when you perform these rituals regularly with colleagues or team members, they also provide a sense of closeness, cohesion, and depth. Rituals can help facilitate and satisfy that sense of belonging that we all crave. And especially when there's a major change or shift (like a global pandemic, for instance) or when there's been a change in leadership or a loss for the company, keep your old rituals going to provide a sense of normalcy, continuity, and grounding for the team.

In your routines that you are establishing with others, it's important to pay attention to whether the actions you're taking are engendering a sense of depth and connection, or whether they are zapping the very connection you are aspiring to create, as technology can frequently do. To combat that, Keswin suggests that we never forget to check in on a personal level: How is this person you're following up with doing in their real, human life? Just because something has become routine (a daily text thread, for instance) doesn't necessarily make it worth repeating. Every once in a while, carefully reevaluate the routines and rituals that you have in your life, and weigh their value in adding depth to your relationships. As you do so, ask yourself: could the medium for this ritual change? Could a weekly team video chat be transformed into an outdoor picnic once a month, for instance?

FIND THEIR CDF
(CHIEF DIFFERENTIATING FACTOR)

I like to think that each person has what I call a chief differentiating factor, or CDF. I see it as each person's *specific expertise or "secret sauce"* that makes them unique. For example, my very dear friend Lisa Witter, cofounder and chair of Apolitical, has a secret sauce that I have admired for years—her sheer command of language. She is one of the most articulate human beings I have ever met. This speciality has enabled to her to command the attention of large audiences, score meetings with global government leaders, and raise millions of dollars from investors who believe in her mission. As you pay more attention to the depth and quality of your relationships, ask yourself: What is this person's chief differentiating factor? In an earlier stage of the relationship, you sought to learn their Oscars introduction, which is simply a few bullet points, the highlight reel of their life and work. But now we want to go deeper: What is this person's unique asset or set of characteristics? Once you learn what someone's CDF is, it's your job to *remind them of it*. If you reflect back on someone's specialness in a way that they can clearly see it—they will be forever grateful. The rewards for both of you will be huge. But if you haven't the first clue what the other person's best assets are, it could be that you don't know them well enough. But it may also be that you simply haven't asked the right questions or truly listened as they responded.

Consider this question: How are you? Now consider this one: What two words best describe how you are feeling today? Brené Brown, author of *Dare to Lead* and the famous researcher who made vulnerability a household name, used this trick to check in with her colleagues during the coronavirus lockdown. On Zoom, her teammates were asked to simply type two words that best described how they were feeling.[11] Instead of getting a chorus of "fine" or "good" in response to the question "How are you?" she received words like *exhausted, terrified, depressed, numb,* or *anxious.* But she also saw words like *hopeful, optimistic,* and *grateful.* The key here lies in how the question was asked. Brown went deeper by asking the right question. On her podcast Unlocking Us, she said, "What I'm seeing right now are these weird paradoxical feelings and emotions." And that's often the case. We love our family *and* they make us frustrated. Deep love and intense frustration can happen at the same time. We can feel both passionate about and exhausted by our work. Communicating in that way with your team—and making space for that kind of dialogue—will no doubt deepen your connection.

My guess is that Brown's team felt pretty seen and heard, and in turn, felt like their relationship with their boss was meaningful, collaborative, and constructive. Over Zoom and other online meeting platforms, since you can't read body language or even see clues like tired-looking eyes or a bright expression, it's important to take these extra emotionally intelligent steps to check in with people in a meaningful way. And as you do, the opportunity to *see* and *understand* people is greater. With an exercise like the one Brown used with her team, the nuances of each person's personality can begin to emerge—and you can begin to see what makes people tick. You can see their specialness, their CDF. And when you can reveal that to them—especially during a challenging time or when that person might struggle to see the full scope of their own value—I promise you they will never forget it.

BECOME A JACK OF ALL TRADES

Let's say you interviewed for a new job or met with a potential new customer. It went flawlessly. But you still got a "no" for the position or to the business. This person doesn't want to become a partner, doesn't want to buy your product, or doesn't want to hire you. Is it time to move on from the relationship? I'd argue no. Don't write them off. One of the greatest things you can do, in addition to finding a way to make each person feel seen, is also to *see* each person you meet as a potential teacher. It used to be a common belief that going deep on one subject (whether it was tennis, finance, or brain surgery) was the best way to become highly successful. Research is now showing the benefit of being a "jack of all trades." Every single person is an expert at something that they could share with you, possibly a topic or skill that you know nothing about that could benefit not only your career, but your life. If you stay open to what this person could potentially share with you, it can bring you closer and also sharpen your professional skillset. Two hundred years ago it was considered good practice to be a "renaissance (wo)man" and know a little about a lot of things. But that's no longer the case. We've become highly specialized. But the tides are starting to shift as people are starting to realize the benefits of a wide range of knowledge, and research is backing this up.

In his book *Range: Why Generalists Triumph in a Specialized World*, David Epstein makes the case that specialization is not the best route to success. While one study found that early career specializers did get a financial jump straight out of college, late specializers caught up to that lead by finding careers that better matched their skills and personality. Epstein also found a slew of studies showing that compared to peers who drilled into one area of expertise, technological inventors increased their creative impact by the experiences they accumulated in different domains. Over and over again he found that your range of past experience was not a detriment, but instead a benefit. And the same could be said of the breadth of the people you know. What the "range" that Epstein alludes to is the breadth of your experiences—which can add further value to your pursuits in business, in sports, and as Epstein argues, even in parenting. People love to share the knowledge and expertise they have with others. You should look at each and every follow-up you execute as an opportunity to widen your range—even if it's with someone who passed on your business or your employment. In his book, Epstein argues that no knowledge is ever wasted—we are, in a sense, continually building upon everything we've ever learned. I would argue the same is true of relationships: we are a compilation of everyone we've ever met. The people you meet along your career will continue to add to your breadth of knowledge and not one encounter—even a negative one—is wasted. Steve Jobs famously said something similar about his study of calligraphy, a seemingly unrelated sidebar to his pursuits in technology. Long before he was a tech icon, Jobs sat in on Robert Palladino's calligraphy class at Portland's Reed College, which eventually inspired the elegant design of Apple computers, as Jobs famously recalled in his 2005 commencement address at Stanford University:[12]

> If I had never dropped out, I would have never dropped in on this calligraphy class, and personal computers might not have the wonderful typography that they do. Of course it was impossible to connect the dots looking forward when I was in college. But it was very, very clear looking backwards ten years later.

You never know how your constellation might unfold in the future and how the relationships and exposures you have along the way may impact your career infinite ways. Stay open to the possibilities—even among the employers who rejected you or the colleagues with whom you don't immediately see a connection—and you may find yourself connecting the dots looking back once your constellation comes into clearer focus.

EXPRESS GRATITUDE

Think for a second about all of the different contacts you've made in your lifetime at virtual or in-person gatherings. You likely have a gigantic list full of professors, colleagues, friends, cofounders, neighbors, and even relatives. Include them all in your mental tally. Now pick the one, two, or three people who have made the biggest impact on your career or on your life. Have you told any of these individuals about the esteemed position they hold in your life? (If you have already told them—has it been a while since you did so?) Now think about a new connection, someone that you met more recently. Have you told that person how grateful you are to know them? Have you ever tried writing a handwritten note to someone who did something for you in your career or in life? Doing so will not only strengthen your ties to that person, it will also give you the warm buzz of happiness and deep connection. I always keep stamps close nearby so that when I think about writing someone—I can do it.

On the flip side, when people reach out to you, acknowledge them. If they do something for you, it is absolutely tantamount that you thank them. In the sea of mass emails we all get—and don't want—a handwritten note will *not* go unnoticed. It will boost feelings of gratitude for you as well as the recipients.

NEVER STOP BEING CURIOUS

Curiosity is linked to psychological, physical, and emotional health. Recent research shows that it may also play a critical role in our social relationships. It makes sense that curious people may have an easier time bonding with a diverse range of people, simply because they are interested in learning about what people from different walks of life have to offer. But can curiosity be learned? Can you become more curious? The research isn't clear. But I would argue that simply walking into a meeting, event, or dinner with the mindset that your primary goal is to find out *about others*—just that reframing of your intentions alone—can make a big difference. If we can learn better stress-reduction and productivity skills in the workplace, why not curiosity? What research *does* show is that from an outsider's perspective, curious people are perceived as more interesting when they engage with others.[13] Curious people do tend to be better connectors in the first place, as research has also shown that curiosity has a link to intimacy scores, which implies that it may aid in facilitating closeness. As Dale Carnegie, author of the book *How to Win Friends and Influence People,* famously wrote:

> You can make more friends in two months by becoming interested in other people than you can in two years by trying to get other people interested in you.

Another study found that people who are more curious might be more skilled at "reading" other people.[14] Studies have also found that people who are curious are better able to navigate negative situations in relationships, too, looking at them as a puzzle to figure out rather than a reason to be offended.[15] Curious people tend to be less aggressive, too, perhaps for the same reasons.[16] When you are open to the possibility of considering different viewpoints, there is not as much potential hostility. With each relationship you develop, ask yourself: What is there to be learned? If you're sitting across from someone vying for a new job, even if they ultimately say no, ask yourself: What other new knowledge could I walk away with? What viewpoint had I been missing? If you're just spewing information about yourself, not only have you not learned anything about the other person, but you haven't deepened the relationship, either.

Whether it's your first tea with someone or your 500th, tuning in to them, to what makes their star shine will not only make that person feel special, but it will also begin to illuminate the pattern of the constellation that you might create together. That pattern when viewed from a far-off distance will create something powerful and bright.

SPREAD THE WEALTH

It may come as a surprise that money can engender connection. But whether it's talking about money (hello, vulnerability) or putting your dollars where your passions are, even the tricky territory of giving, receiving, or talking about money, when used skillfully, can pave the way to greater closeness. First, by financially supporting businesses you care about, you can build meaningful connections. Whether it's a small contribution to a crowdfunding site or a larger investment in a business, putting your money behind the organizations and people you want to support is a great way to build relationships in a truly meaningful way. You truly don't need to have a large savings account to do this. Just 10 dollars to a crowdsourced campaign could connect you to an organization you may care about for life, and that can introduce you to fascinating people. Similarly, every frank and open conversation you're willing to have about money is another way to engender depth, openness, and transparency in your business relationships, too. When we can have tough conversations about hard things, a feeling of closeness emerges, and talking about tricky subjects like money can facilitate deep connections. Whether you're asking for money or offering to provide it, discussing how much you earn or how much you charge for your services, even the most skilled negotiators can trip up during conversations around money.

INVEST IN PEOPLE

Ten years ago, after the loss of both of my parents, I realized that I had some disposable income on my hands due to a modest inheritance as well as the class action lawsuit that occurred after the tragic death of my mother. Without kids to put through college, I realized that I could use this money to support the great work of women, elevate their voices, and help other organizations hoping to do the same. And as I've said all along: if you take action to support organizations that you care about, the relationships will happen organically. When you are surrounded by people with a common purpose and a shared set of values, those sparks will ignite. I spent many years, and still do, donating to nonprofit organizations and volunteering my time. But I soon realized that investing in female-founded businesses was another way to champion and support women, and to further advance the causes I cared about.

According to the Center for Venture Research, in 2016, only 26 percent of US angel investors were women, and only 5 percent were minorities.[1] But in my research, I came across organizations like Golden Seeds, which is one of the largest and most active angel networks that focuses on women-led businesses and has invested over 120 million dollars in over 170 companies across a diverse range of industries. 37 Angels is also a community of female investors. Pipeline Angels is changing the face of angel investing and creating capital for women and nonbinary femme social entrepreneurs. I realized in my research that becoming an angel investor not only was a way to support causes that I passionately cared about, but would also create more jobs for women—a social good that I have always valued. When I spoke to Fran Hauser about her established career as an investor, she said that as a funder, it gave her a means through which to share her wisdom and expertise as a long-time media executive. When I started out investing, I set my criteria to fund only women entrepreneurs who have created an innovative product or service, and to focus on those who could benefit from the support of my network or advice in addition to my financial contribution.

In this way, the power of connecting continues. Over the years, I have been able to connect people in a synergistic way that helps these burgeoning businesses grow. Rather than just waiting for a check, I enjoy having a seat at the table to share my business knowledge, my community, and my experience. Even if I don't earn a return on these investments—though that's certainly one of the goals—these investments have provided returns to me in enormous ways by introducing me to people and allowing me to learn a great deal about a wide range of growing businesses. All have proven to be extraordinary opportunities. On paper, what I have given these female founders may have gone to fund hiring, technology platforms, or expansion into new markets. But if you were to ask any of the women that I've supported, my guess is that they would tell you that what they valued most about my involvement wasn't the money, but the relationships that they developed through our connection.

HOW INVESTING WORKS

Angel investing is giving seed funding to early-stage startups before they are ready to raise venture capital money. It used to be a practice that was restricted to high-net-worth individuals, but since the passage of the Jumpstart Our Business Startups Act in 2012, it is now more accessible for investors wanting to make a smaller investment.[2] The Jumpstart Our Business Startups Act was a law passed with the intention of encouraging funding for small businesses, by easing some of the security regulations in the United States. In 2015, the Securities and Exchange Commission also adopted the final rules allowing equity crowdfunding, known as the Crowdfund Act.[3] Essentially, this law made it legal for startups to raise money in small chunks from a large number (i.e., the crowd) of nonaccredited investors. Since Pipeline Angels launched in April 2011, close to 400 members have graduated from their angel investing program and have invested more than $6 million in over 70 companies via their pitch summit process.

With such a low percentage of female angel investors, companies are missing out on benefiting from the unique skills that women bring to the table, such as inspiring collaboration between disparate groups and targeting the female consumer market. After all, women make 75 to 85 percent of all purchasing decisions, and their impact on the global economy is growing exponentially.[4] It only makes sense that more female investors as well as investors of color need to be brought to the table and into the conversation to facilitate change.

BENEFITS OF ANGELS

As I dug in, I learned that females and minorities are drastically underrepresented in funding. Not only are there few female and minority investors, but only a small amount of the funding goes to them as well. Only about 2 percent of venture capital goes to women.[5] And if you even peel that back more, far less goes to women of color. I started thinking: *Wait, I could do both, right?* Investing gets you a seat at the table and gives you an opportunity to learn about a new industry that maybe you weren't familiar with.

IFundWomen is a startup funding platform providing access to capital through crowdfunding and grants, as well as offering a network for support and expert business coaching. Women are starting new businesses at a rate of almost five times greater than the national average. However, females struggle to land funding capital without going into debt. Only 1 percent of all startup businesses will receive funding—regardless of founder's gender or race. So it's a daunting challenge to begin with that is made only more challenging for women and founders of color. What differentiates IFundWomen is its proprietary coaching program, the IFundwomen method, which supports women by offering capital, connections, and coaching—three key elements in startup launch that are needed today.

DISPEL AWKWARDNESS AROUND MONEY

Another important element in the conversation about money and relationships is this idea that what we earn defines our identity. We need to drop some of the stories about self-worth that surround money and instead—we need to start sharing what we are paid in our communities with friends and colleagues to ensure transparency and support across industries. As much as you can, proactively bring people together in your network to have conversations around money. Linda Davis Taylor is the former CEO and chairman of Clifford Swan Investment Counselors in Pasadena, California. She currently writes for *Worth* magazine, and a longtime advocate for women's financial independence and frequently speaks on the topics of wealth and philanthropy. As one of our clients at McPherson Strategies we helped Linda create Money Talks, which is like a sewing circle or book club gathering to talk about money, and most recently a podcast called *Money Stories with LDT*, which expands on this idea. Instead of playing mahjong or bridge, Money Talks bring people together to talk about what you're paid and how to advocate for more, which is helping bring transparency to an area often defined by secrets. Hosting a Money Talk is an opportunity to convene the knowledge and experience of your network. It can also create a system of accountability as we individually set out to reach our own personal finance goals. Bring the power of connection into our financial lives and build our confidence and competence as a community—it can be as small as two people.

Here are some jumping-off points for kickstarting a conversation about money. Like the relationship-deepening questions we discussed earlier, these are also great questions to add to your conversational toolkit to spark deeper and more meaningful discussions in your daily life:

- How did you learn about money growing up?
- What do you think society tells women (or doesn't tell women) about financial planning?
- When did you start to feel confident in managing your own personal finances?
- What was the most valuable money lesson you learned from a parent or guardian?

- When you envision having "enough" money to live, what is that vision?
- What is your personal reaction to the concept of wealth and growing your money?
- What is your approach to savings?
- What is your perspective on charitable giving? Your perspective on investing?
- Do you have a "rainy-day" fund? Emergency fund?
- What is your approach to debt?
- What are your feelings toward "splurging"?

HOW TO ASK FOR IT

Let's say you're getting a new business off the ground. How do you ask for funding? Let's first ask why you need the funding. Now there are these great vehicles, whether it's Kickstarter or iFundWomen.com where you can raise that first 20, or 30, or 40,000 dollars. Yes, it's hard work. Don't get me wrong. But that could get you to a place where you would have some cushion to bring on a programmer or a consultant to create your websites and your collateral. When you have deep, meaningful relationships, it's a lot easier to generate support if you've already built the types of relationships you will need to fund your company. Any kind of campaign on a platform like iFundWomen could be so much more successful if you have already put the time and energy into building meaningful relationships.

BEYOND INVESTING

While writing her book *The Myth of the Nice Girl*, Fran Hauser created what she calls the Nice Girl Army. This is a group of women Hauser had previously mentored and she gathered them together to amplify the message of her book. These gatherings grew into mentoring, networking sessions, parties, and workshops. This is a great example of how what can start as an investment relationship can turn into something much more—these women came to the groups to meet Fran, but they ended up meeting each other and developing relationships in a more streamlined but also incredibly effective way, in groups of six to eight people rather than one-on-one. In that way, the investor and investee or even mentor and mentee relationship can expand, grow, and evolve outside the bounds of what you "expected" the form of that relationship might take. It's also a great example of how what seems like the best scenario for a relationship (one-on-one) might not actually be the best. Stay open to all of the possibilities of what can happen when you invest in and with people and causes you care about.

NOT FOR PROFIT

As someone who works in corporate responsibility (read: help-ing companies improve their environmental, social, and philanthropic effects on their constituents), and as a woman busi-ness owner, it can be hard to differentiate at times between what is a favor/free advice versus what is a paid service. And when your circles of friends and colleagues overlap in all the good ways we've explored, that line is even blurrier when drinks turns into a strat-egy meeting, or vice versa. This chapter offers guidelines to assert when what you share is a moneymaker and when it's for free. The most successful people I know toe this line with the finesse of Fred Astaire, and no one is ever insulted in the process.

NEVER SAY NEVER

At some point in your life, you may come face-to-face with a cause that you care so much about that you *have* to take action. For me, this was the Don't Ban Equality campaign in 2019. At the time, Donald Trump was three years into his presidency, abortion bans were being passed in several states, and the stability and stamina of the laws that protected a woman's right to choose were liter-ally being threatened. So at McPherson Strategies, we worked with NARAL Pro-Choice America, the American Civil Liberties Union, and Planned Parenthood to rally company CEOs to come together and say, "Don't Ban Equality—We won't stand for this. You can't take away reproductive rights because that will take away women's autonomy and ability to progress and have equality in the workplace." At first, we were told that companies would never make a statement like that. We were told by countless numbers that no company would sign on to any statement containing the word *abortion*—ever. Well, they were wrong.

Because I'd worked in corporate responsibility for so long and had built up my constellation of contacts who cared about these same equal rights as I do—it was slightly easier to reach out to the right people, efficiently, and make this happen. I connected my team to my corporate friends and colleagues who worked in policy or corporate responsibility at major companies. We had conversations with all of them to learn where they stood on this issue and provided polling data from the general public as well as the workforce. We pressed them on their position and how they felt and on the importance of that moment in female reproductive rights. Because of those conversations, and also as a result of the long-term relationships that I had built, we were able to showcase 180 company CEOs who signed a letter that was placed in the *New York Times* stating that the abortion bans were bad for business and bad for equality. Within one week, an addition 178 CEOs joined the campaign.

One key reason this succeeded was because I wasn't reaching out to these contacts cold. I'd been sending them interesting articles, seeing them at events, and retweeting their comments on social platforms for years. And so it goes back to my father's advice to "never wait until you need something from someone to do something for them." I'd become a trusted resource for them, and as a result, I not only knew the right people to ask, but I'd built in a foundation of trust. The people I called on this issue listened—and together we made that *New York Times* ad happen.

PRACTICE EXPERTISE AMNESIA

Sometimes, you just need to forget what it is you thought you needed and take action *where* and *how* you can—especially in a crisis. In many instances in this book, I've talked about the importance of figuring out your constellation according to your unique set of skills and experiences. But sometimes the opportunity to join a circle of people in a meaningful way will appear right before your eyes—if you are willing to dive in and help those around you, particularly in an emergency. This is precisely what happened to Rachel Gerrol Cohen, who is widely recognized for her work on innovative philanthropy. She was named one of the "99 Most Influential Foreign Policy Leaders under 33" by the Diplomatic Courier. Gerrol is also CEO and cofounder of NEXUS, a global community founded to bridge communities of wealth and social entrepreneurship. With over 6,000 members from 70 countries, the organization works to unite young investors, social entrepreneurs, philanthropists, and allies to catalyze new leadership and accelerate needed political, societal, indigenous, financial, environmental, and equal justice solutions. Gerrol also lives by the ethos of asking, "What can we do together" rather than "What can you do for me?"

Nexus's response to hurricane Dorian is a great example. It was really about the strength of the community. When hurricane Dorian hit the Bahamas, it largely demolished Abaco Islands in the Grand Bahamas, creating 20 feet of standing water for two days. People were standing on their rooftops, waiting to be rescued or hoping that the water would recede. Every single vehicle, plane, and truck on that island was destroyed. Since the area was flooded, the prime minister established a no-fly zone, and the NEXUS team sent five Black Hawk helicopters and private planes during that first 24 hours, pulling over 1,000 people off of their rooftops. They also put out a call to members for small boats that could be used to bring over the relief workers who were coming from organizations like UNICEF. A couple of days later, when Gerrol arrived on the ground in the Bahamas, she says there were people wearing NEXUS shirts everywhere. She was so confused: she hadn't given anyone the logo. But people had quickly jumped in to help. No one said, "Oh, I'm not a relief worker. I can't help." They just rolled up their sleeves and started making things happen.

Whether it's a crisis or not—there's often this sense that you have to have a certain level of expertise before you can offer something or make an ask. This is why I like to share this anecdote about Gerrol and NEXUS and the great work they did in the Bahamas. The people who accomplish extraordinary things and build meaningful relationships in doing so—the ones who really can change the world—don't wait for permission. They dive right in. Many of the people who helped save thousands of lives from those Bahamian rooftops didn't have any relief work experience or any connection to the Bahamas at all. Someone just asked, "Can I borrow your boat to help?" And they said yes.

ALIGN WITH PEOPLE AND PASSION—NOT PROJECTS

Have you ever heard the adage: "You are the average of the five people you spend the most time with"? In his book *The Art of Exceptional Living*, motivational speaker John Rohn famously shared this insight, along with tips and insights on how to employ self-education to change your life. Research shows that we are *heavily* influenced by the people in our orbit, particularly those with whom we spend the most time.[1] Our chosen circle of contacts can influence everything from professional outcomes to whether we gain weight, who we find attractive, or how many cocktails we drink. I take Rohn's advice one step further: surround yourself with people you find *inspiring and continue to spark your curiosity*—even if their passions and pursuits have little to do with your career goals.

Every few months, take a brief assessment of your community. Who are you exposed to? What events do you get an invitation to? Do these people inspire you? If not, immerse yourself in the world of the ones *who do*. You don't need permission to get to know someone who inspires you—reach out to *those* people, insert yourself in those events even the ones held online. When you do, offers and asks will fly organically—and you won't be left watching from afar.

Ginny Suss has long followed this advice to significant effect. Suss emerged as one of the founders and producers of the Women's March worldwide protest on January 21, 2017, the day after Donald Trump was inaugurated as president. It became the largest single-day protest in US history.[2] When I asked Suss to share how she landed in that pivotal role, she said it was primarily the result of her decision to align with inspiring people doing important work. The day after Trump was elected president of the United States, a woman by the name of Teresa Shook of Hawaii created a Facebook event and invited friends to march on Washington in protest. Soon similar Facebook pages emerged, and practically overnight, thousands of women were signed up to march. These women decided to consolidate their pages, and soon the official Women's March on Washington was established. At the time, Vanessa Wruble was cofounder and copresident of Okayafrica with Suss and later served as the head of campaign operations for the Women's March. Suss says that when Wruble first told her about the concept of the March, there was no real structure or even a real name. Still, she felt passionate about connecting and collaborating with women in that moment of political crisis. Because she was already woven into the fabric of that community, there was not a formal ask, but more of a friendly, "Hey—do you want to work on this together?" These are the best kinds of asks to make (or get). Not everyone has that privilege or that opportunity, but as much as you can, be proactive about building that skill.

Suss took on the same strategy when she built the Resistance Revival Chorus (RRC), now a collective of more than 60 women who join together to breathe joy and song into the resistance, and to uplift and center women's voices. After the Women's March, a few women from the creative team had an idea: they wanted to come together and sing protest music. Suss put a call out to her network of musicians in New York with a straightforward ask: "Do you want to get together and sing—to revive the spirit of music in this movement?" She didn't expect many people to respond. She had no budget or promises of what may come. But since people trusted her and felt aligned with her mission and knew her creative genius, they wanted in. When they first got together in a friend's small Manhattan living room, Suss says she couldn't believe how many showed up. There was collective energy, a buzz. It was clear that something powerful was forming. And from there, it just snowballed. Women were singing, protesting, connecting, being heard—challenging the systems and structures of power. Suss says the glue, the most potent magnetic force that held everything together, was the connection and network of women—passionate women aligned by a cause.

What started in a friend's overflowing living room has blossomed into a group that has performed at Carnegie Hall. These women exude passion and belt out righteous music—ballads infused with protest, love, connection, and a sharp critique of the cultural systems of power and race. It's stunning to behold. The songs fill everyone with joy and hope. It all started with a simple ask.

Suss says that the members of the chorus often return to the saying, "Joy is an act of resistance." She says that human beings can be oppressed and stripped bare, but you will always have joy; you'll always have your voice. Maybe your passion isn't singing, but fighting for refugee rights. Or perhaps you feel most passionate about removing bias in journalism or eliminating poverty. Whatever your passion is—find *those* people, the ones creating waves in *that* space. And in those instances, the asks will be organic.

ALWAYS TAKE
(AND INNOVATE ON)
THE MEETING

"Always take the meeting" is a quip that runs through many networking guides. It is a testament to what we're talking about in this book; you'll never know where a connection will lead, even it takes you somewhere you didn't expect. But I like to take this advice one step further, encouraging you to constantly push yourself to innovate on what "meetings" even mean, in addition to saying yes to potential meetings as much as you can (without burning out, of course).

CONTINUE TO INNOVATE ON
THE MEETING ITSELF

While I do embrace the ethos of "always take the meeting," I also like to continue to innovate on what meetings can—and should—even look like. Yes, a cup of coffee is a nice way to have a business or even a personal chat. But I feel that as human beings, we've only scratched the surface on how we can connect with each other in a meaningful way—especially when it comes to remote, digital connections. Just as it's easy to get stuck in our familiar social circles, or get caught in a ritual rut, doing the same routine habits over and over, so too it's possible to hold the same type of meetings, or fail to innovate on the best format for connection. Human beings are great at innovating in response to constraints, however, so it's no surprise that 2020 saw a surge of innovation in the way that gatherings and meetings occur. I encourage each of us to not only stay open and curious about the people with whom we connect and bring into the fold of our lives and work, but also the ways in which we see each other.

Priya Parker is a master facilitator, strategic adviser, and acclaimed author of *The Art of Gathering: How We Meet and Why It Matters*. Like me, Parker is a serial connector, and she's dedicated her career to examining and understanding how human beings best connect. When I asked her to weigh in on the surge of meeting innovation that we saw in 2020, here's what she told me:

> We are in a moment, where through necessity, millions of people are using tools that weren't built for the purposes they are now using them for. Zoom was originally intended as a business tool for business meetings. But, we are now seeing people using it for everything from defending dissertations to making Passover to underground all-night raves. We are also seeing an eruption of new digital tools to try and solve problems that Zoom isn't good for. For example, because of the algorithm in Zoom that tries to elevate one voice to avoid total chaos, it's problematic for something like virtual choir rehearsals.

Just as I say that everyone is an invitation to something else, I also feel that every new mode of communication or gathering is an opportunity to learn something about how human beings operate and thrive. While I may not use *every* tool that emerges this year or in the rest of my lifetime, I remain curious about all of the creative ways human beings forge connections and encourage you to do the same. While we've already covered the most common tools like

Zoom, Slack, and email, did you know that there are hundreds of other platforms and tools for connecting? What if you're using Slack because that's what you're most familiar with, but an entirely different tool might better serve your specific project or community?

According to Commsor, a platform for community builders, about 45 percent of the tools in our ecosystem are less than three years old! Just as the postal service, email, cell phones, and texts changed our lives and exploded the possibility for human connection (as well as offered new challenges and new ways to disconnect, too), imagine the possibilities that lay ahead for us and for future generations. It's worth innovating and asking the question: What am I not doing? How am I not reaching others in ways that I should? And whether you're the person who creates technology or simply uses it, asking how we can best show up for each other as humans is a worthwhile exploration. Keep your eyes open for new platforms for connection, and be willing to try them out, even the new or unpopular ones.

HELP YOUR NEIGHBOR

With the "always take the meeting" ethos, one might have the idea that your constellation will include only the people you'll run into in a business suit. But what about the very people who *are* your neighbors? Have you ever thought about them as potential business leads? Or people to bring into your orbit for later professional collaboration? Just as I say you never know where a contact might take you and don't be afraid to innovate on the good old-fashioned meeting, I also recommend that you keep your eyes peeled for fruitful connections at every possible turn, even at the mailbox. If you think about it, it makes sense that you may wish to connect with those who live closest to you—and since I profess that work and life aren't separate, why not do business with your neighbors? But somewhere along the way in recent American history, we stopped connecting with our neighbors. We began to refrain from asking for a cup of sugar or a spare egg. For insights on how that evolved and how people tend to connect (or fail to do so) with their neighbors today, I turned to Maryam Banikarim, head of marketing for Nextdoor, the popular app that connects you to the people who live in your neighborhood. First I was curious about how Nextdoor came to be and what that might say about how neighbors relate to each other. When I asked Banikarim what inspired the creation of Nextdoor, here's what she told me:

> One of the founders of Nextdoor read an article that referenced a Pew study talking about how many people at that time didn't know a single one of their neighbors. They thought, "Wow, how could I leverage technology to solve for *that*?" And unlike some of the other social platforms, where they want you to spend immense amounts of time on the platform itself, Nextdoor was created as a means to an end—a vehicle for connecting you with people nearby, so that you can actually meet face-to-face and have more human connections.

So Nextdoor, like many of the tools, programs, nonprofits, and companies we've discussed in this book, was created to solve a pressing social problem. That disconnect I mentioned in our everyday neighborhoods—people were fragmented, cut off from their neighbors, no longer dropping by to offer that they could pick up the mail while you were out of town. What's amazing too is how Nextdoor as a connecting tool works even in a city like New York, where people don't always get the reputation of being neighborly or even friendly! When I asked Banikarim about the connections she's seen transpire in Manhattan specifically, she told me the story of a woman who'd just moved to the city and posted, "I'm Brazilian, I'm 50 and I'm a producer and it's hard to make new friends—I'd really just like to meet some new people." Banikarim said that by the end of the week, she had over 140 replies to her post! People responded to say where they worked out, where they went for meditation, and even offered their phone numbers and emails. There were real friendships and community emerging from that simple request, and she's seen it time and time again on the platform. Who knows what career moves or professional projects may have also emerged from that 100+ list of fellow neighbors. At the very least, that producer likely felt very seen and supported in her new city of New York.

The goal of those Nextdoor posts is to bring people together in real life, where someone might connect you to a potential new employer, a new idea, or something totally unexpected. It's worth asking yourself if you're staying open to all of the different possibilities in your life where connections could transpire: Are there avenues of connections that have become blocked off for one reason or another, as the traditional neighborly chat did over time? And as you build your constellation, don't forget to think about the people who live right within your own zip code. Even if only for an occasional Jeep drive-by or a brief sighting of a taco on roller skates—who wouldn't love that?

THE POSSIBILITY IN A
LAST-MINUTE STOP

What further differentiates the way I view "always take the meeting" from how it's typically viewed in traditional networking manuals is perhaps my fervent belief in the power and magic—the beautiful serendipity and synchronicity—that can happen even in the day to day. Just as you might unexpectedly make a connection at the mailbox, if you stay open to it, you may also do the same while you're out making a last-minute purchase. In this case, "always take the meeting" really means, perpetually having your meeting hat on. I don't mean always be working, rather, keep the possibility of a fortuitous connection afloat in your mind. One example of this comes from Brandt Anderson, a film director and producer known for films such as *Everest*, *The Flowers of War*, and most recently the short film *Refugee*. His work with refugees and the relationships that have transpired as a result are the perfect illustration of how the magic of the constellation effect can occur when you do work that you love and stay open to taking the meeting no matter what shape or form it appears in—even while you're in the checkout line.

Anderson first became involved with refugees in 2010 after the earthquake in Haiti, when he arrived three days after that quake and spent several weeks there working with Haitians who had become eco refugees. In 2012, he began working with Syrian refugees shortly after the start of the Syrian civil war. Over his career working with refugees, Anderson found doors opening to some of the most meaningful and amazing relationships of his life, with refugees, aid workers, actors, and even heads of state. When I asked him for an example of how these relationships transpired and how staying open to the idea of always take the meeting translated into meaningful connections, this is what he said:

> I met Angela Mwanza, the cofounder of UBS's Evergreen Management team, on a bus in Tulum, Mexico. In our five-minute bus ride we made a meaningful connection and exchanged information so that we could stay in touch. From that short bus ride Angela introduced me to you, Susan, then you introduced me to CARE—CARE then asked me to lead a filmmaking boot camp for refugee children living in the Azraq refugee camp in Jordan. That boot camp led to a life-changing experience for the Los Angeles filmmakers leading the camp as well as the kids who learned to share their personal stories through film.

That's quite a series of connections from that one bus ride! It literally changed the lives of the refugee kids who were able to take that boot camp and no doubt made a meaningful impact on the lives of everyone involved throughout that particular constellation—through the relationships and *actions* that transpired as a result.

When I asked Anderson about the most surprising connections he's made and how it transpired, he told me the story of a last-minute purchase he made before leaving the country one time, that facilitated an incredible friendship:

> I was headed to a Middle Eastern country to work with refugees.
> I was grabbing a shirt at a local store in my town the day before

traveling. I mentioned to the sales associate that I was off to this particular country and in passing said that I had been trying to connect to the Royal Family to let them know of my plans while in the country. The sales associate said, "That's funny, the King of that country was just in here and I have his cell number." The next morning I was on a call with the King and he has since become a great friend.

While you may not meet a king as a result of any last-minute trips to the convenience store, you will no doubt make an untold number of friends, colleagues, collaborators, and partners in similar instances where you will be in some place for *one* thing, but make a connection that can help or segue into an entirely different thing all together. Trust me. This has happened to me on numerous occasions. As you continue to build your constellation, I encourage you to break all the meeting rules: who you might connect with, how, with what platform, and even when. In fact, those are the most fun connections of all time—when they are truly serendipitous and unexpected. And so too this makes the art of connecting one of the most engaging and exciting parts of my life, and now, I hope yours, too. You never know who might be just around the corner, waiting to join your constellation—if you are present and open to the opportunity.

DO REVIEW: WHAT WE'VE LEARNED

The final stage in solidifying your constellation is dependent on your actions: the *Do* part of my three-part approach. There's a reason why "all talk and no action" is a common expression. To establish a meaningful connection—in life and especially in business— you have to be someone who gets things done. This is important. Regardless of where or how you met someone, follow up, deepen the relationship—right after you meet them. You can simply write to say, "Let's stay in touch." Or "I'd like to follow the work you're doing and get to know you better." People greatly appreciate radical transparency and honesty.

Your next task: help the other person feel seen, safe, and secure. If you can find people's uniqueness or "secret sauce," what I call their "chief differentiating factor" and *show* it to them, they'll never forget it. And as you continue to have conversations with your constellation of contacts, keep finding ways to make the conversation deeper. Resist the safe bet, the small talk; I even dare you to talk about money! Ask others more questions that will open the possibility for greater closeness and intimacy, like "What's something you've long dreamed of doing but haven't?" And finally, draw yourself closer and solidify the pattern of your constellation by creating rituals, expressing gratitude, remaining curious, and being utterly generous with your support, even with your wallet And when people need help—jump in to give it! There's no greater feeling in the world than feeling deeply listened to, fiercely supported, and intimately seen and known. And when you do that for the people in your constellation, they will offer it back. And the pattern you make together will be sealed for good.

EPILOGUE

As I've said all along, when you live life according to *The Lost Art of Connecting*, you can make your life work and your work your life. It can all blend together into one big shining constellation, because it doesn't quite feel like *work* when it's meaningful. I laugh when people tell me what will be written on my tombstone: *She got sh*t done.*

Yes, that's partially true.

But as the Beatles so famously sang, I did it with a little help from my friends. Because if you pay attention to and cherish the people you meet at those various pitstops along your life's path, you will create enduring friendships. And if you are human, vulnerable, and kind—people will be much more willing to support you in the good as well as the more challenging moments. Remember, it's so often the detours rather than the destination that matters most.

When I pause to take stock of the constellation of meaningful connections that I have developed in my lifetime, I feel enormous gratitude. For those who have guided and supported me, for those whom I've helped and connected, and for those that I've yet to meet. Each day, I feel those connections in my life. Phone calls, emails, text messages, online meetings, WhatsApp chats—they all nourish me daily. In the course of an average day, I hear from so many different people in my life. And each communication brings me a sense of joy and satisfaction. I feel as though the work we've done together and the relationships we maintain have meaning, for the world and for me, and that brings me a great sense of happiness and optimism.

As I end the writing of this book during month seven of working from home while living alone, I realize that my virtual connections have been my source of nourishment and tonic during this very peculiar time. They have truly been what has kept me moving forward, remaining hopeful, and continuing to stay focused. By way of closing, I hope to offer some last words of encouragement to stay on this path of service, connection, and valuing people over profit even when society is at odds with these values (to a degree—it all depends on the company you keep). We need that more than ever at this time in history.

It cements my philosophy of "my work is my life, and my life is my work"—in other words, everything I do with my time, every conversation, every relationship is going toward growing the business of my life. I remain steadfast that there is no line between work-Susan and home-Susan, which has allowed me to maintain a sustainable business through all its twists and turns, and is what keeps me confident about what's ahead, but also rested and refreshed. I love what I do and feel inspired each day. I also value rest and relaxation, but my work and my social world are intertwined in extremely positive ways and my energy is rejuvenated each time I'm surrounded by those working in social impact and justice.

And perhaps that is the best advice of all: when you love what you do, and you love who you do it with—there really is no *work* at all.

So I'd like to amend my future tombstone inscription. I'd like to add a nod to the people in my life who've helped me, supported me, and are not just colleagues or coworkers, but friends. *We* got sh*t done.

BERYL SPECTOR'S RECIPE FOR CINNAMON HORNS AND STRUDEL

My late mom's treats served at
every one of her gatherings.

HORNS

1 cup butter (room temperature)

2 cups flour (sifted)

1/8 teaspoon salt

1 8-ounce package cream cheese

Sugar and cinnamon for rolling

1. Preheat oven to 350 degrees Fahrenheit.

2. Mix all the ingredients together and refrigerate dough for at least 3 to 4 hours or overnight.

3. Cut into fourths. Roll each fourth out into a circle on a mixture of sugar and cinnamon instead of flour, and cut into triangles (like pie wedges).

4. Roll up each triangle into a crescent.

5. Bake at 350 or 375 degrees Fahrenheit until golden brown on cookie sheet with parchment paper.

STRUDEL

1 cup butter

2 cups flour

1/8 teaspoon salt

1 cup sour cream

Filling

Jar of your favorite raspberry jam

Golden raisins

Sweetened coconut flakes

Chopped walnuts (if desired)

1. Mix together and refrigerate dough for at least 3 to 4 hours or overnight.

2. Cut into fourths, and roll each fourth into a long rectangle (10 to 12 inches by 6 to 8 inches), using flour to prevent sticking.

3. Spread jam throughout, leaving an inch from edges. Sprinkle with raisins, coconut flakes, and nuts (if desired).

4. Roll up into a log and place on cookie sheet with parchment paper. Repeat three more times.

5. Bake at 350 or 375 degrees until golden brown for approximately 30 minutes. Once cool, slice into 1-inch pieces.

ACKNOWLEDGMENTS

How often do you hear, "it took a village?" Well, writing my book took a very large city! So many played an instrumental and valuable role, but I'll start at the beginning of the journey. Deep gratitude to Lisa Weinert, who (after meeting in an elevator) suggested I write a book, convinced me that I had something to say, and then patiently coached me for far too many months so I could actually commit the words to paper. And I'd be nowhere without my brilliant and kind cowriter, Jackie Ashton.

Thanks also to my agent, Lucinda Halpern, for her guidance and counsel along the way. And to my editor, Amy Li, who believed in me, guided me, and sharpened my words with her deft hand. To my publicists, Barbara Hendricks and Nina Niccolino, whose wise counsel and industry acumen helped the world learn it existed. And to Margaret Biedel, who instilled beauty and joy into the book's cover design. And in no way would the book have been possible without wisdom from the brilliant individuals whom I interviewed for it and who took time out of their busy lives to speak with me: Julian Treasure, Amy Nelson, Tiffany Dufu, Cate Luzio, Paul van Zyl, Gina Pell, Dee Poku, Adam Grant, Erica Keswin, Shiza Shahid, Ginny Suss, Sarah Sophie Flicker, Ruth Ann Harnisch, Mora Aarons-Mele, Rachel Gerrol Cohen, Ali Gelles, Whitney Johnson, Fran Hauser, Cindi Leive, Maryam Banikarim, Priya Parker, Jamia Wilson, Rhonesha Byng, Gina Bianchini, Jennifer DaSilva, Brooke Baldwin, Susan Danziger, Nancy Sells, Baratunde Thurston, Rebecca Soffer, Daisy Auger-Dominguez, Naj Austin, Stacy London, and Laurie Segall. Thank you for the incredible insight, wisdom, and personality you poured into this book—especially during a global pandemic—and for teaching me a thing or two about how to build meaningful relationships. And I would be remiss if I didn't thank my sister, Nancy Spector, who has been by side since we shared a room all those years ago in a little town in upstate New York and managed to not "kill" each other. Back in 2003, it was she who convinced me to move from Seattle to New York City, during a divorce, a city where I knew not a soul and said, "You may be lonely in NYC, but you'll never be alone."

It would take publishing another book to thank all my beloved friends, my team at McPherson Strategies, our clients, the members of the communities I belong to (including The WIE Suite, TheLi.st, Reboot, Morning Sunshines, Kindred, and more), all who have instilled in me a sense of belonging and community, and all the colleagues who have come before in previous lives—but you all played a role in this book's creation.

With that, I will leave you with words I live by. Open that door. No matter how scared you might feel doing it, not knowing what is on the other side, chances are it will change your life for the better.

NOTES

INTRODUCTION
1. https://www.pewresearch.org/internet/2009/11/04/social-isolation-and -new-technology/
2. https://www.forbes.com/sites/neilhowe/2019/05/03/millennials-and-the -loneliness-epidemic/#2021820a7676
3. https://www.hrsa.gov/enews/past-issues/2019/january-17/loneliness -epidemic
4. https://www.nytimes.com/2017/12/11/well/mind/how-loneliness-affects -our-health.html
5. https://www.uchicagomedicine.org/forefront/health-and-wellness -articles/what-is-loneliness
6. https://www.theworldcounts.com/happiness/social-connections-and -happiness

CHAPTER 1
1. https://doi.apa.org/doiLanding?doi=10.1037percent2Fa0038333
2. http://personal.lse.ac.uk/Kanazawa/pdfs/JEP2009.pdf
3. https://www.cigna.com/static/www-cigna-com/docs/about-us /newsroom/studies-and-reports/combatting-loneliness/cigna-2020 -loneliness-report.pdf
4. https://www.nhs.uk/news/mental-health/loneliness-increases-risk-of -premature-death/
5. https://www.usatoday.com/story/news/health/2019/03/07/millennial -generation-z-social-media-connected-loneliness-cigna-health-study /3090013002/
6. https://www.jneurosci.org/content/31/17/6362
7. https://online.olivet.edu/news/research-friends-work
8. https://online.olivet.edu/news/research-friends-work
9. https://hbr.org/2019/07/to-be-happier-at-work-invest-more-in-your -relationships
10. https://www.livescience.com/58935-social-neuropeptides-oxytocin -dopamine-endorphins.html

11. https://www.cnn.com/2009/TECH/10/24/tech.networks.connected /index.html
12. https://www.gartner.com/en/newsroom/press-releases/2018-06-07 -gartner-survey-reveals-connector-manager-approach-bes

CHAPTER 2

1. https://www.fastcompany.com/90374692/how-to-stop-your-people -pleasing-behavior-from-limiting-your-success
2. https://en.wikipedia.org/wiki/Reciprocity_(social_psychology)
3. https://www.npr.org/sections/health-shots/2012/11/26/165570502/give -and-take-how-the-rule-of-reciprocation-binds-us

CHAPTER 3

1. https://www.flexjobs.com/blog/post/remote-work-statistics/
2. https://www.forbes.com/sites/causeintegration/2017/10/04/how -a-culture-of-giving-back-inspires-something-better-than-engagement/ #2ee7903175c1
3. https://www.unitedhealthgroup.com/content/dam/UHG/PDF/2013 /UNH-Health-Volunteering-Study.pdf
4. https://www2.deloitte.com/content/dam/Deloitte/us/Documents/us -deloitte-impact-survey.pdf
5. http://www.villafane.com/wp-content/uploads/2015/11/Cap-7_2014 _Strengthening-Employee-Relationships_Altimeter.pdf
6. https://journals.sagepub.com/doi/abs/10.1177/0956797612442551
7. https://www.smallbizlabs.com/2016/08/coworking-forecast-44-million -members-in-2020.html
8. https://hbr.org/2017/12/coworking-is-not-about-workspace-its-about -feeling-less-lonely
9. https://hbr.org/2017/12/coworking-is-not-about-workspace-its-about -feeling-less-lonely
10. https://www.jstor.org/stable/2776392?seq=1
11. https://www.jstor.org/stable/202051?seq=1
12. https://greatergood.berkeley.edu/article/item/are_some_ties_better _than_others
13. https://www.nber.org/papers/w22596.pdf

CHAPTER 4

1. https://www.fastcompany.com/3051518/the-science-of-when-you-need -in-person-communication
2. https://papers.ssrn.com/sol3/papers.cfm?abstract_id=2443551

3. https://www.fastcompany.com/3051518/the-science-of-when-you-need
   -in-person-communication
4. https://www.nytimes.com/2016/02/28/magazine/what-google-learned
   -from-its-quest-to-build-the-perfect-team.html
5. https://medium.com/@ronenmichael/can-we-create-digital-intimacy-in
   -times-of-physical-distancing-a7d5c754446c
6. https://www.oxford-review.com/oxford-review-encyclopaedia-terms
   /relational-energy-what-it-is-and-why-it-matters-to-organisations/
7. https://hbr.org/2016/09/the-energy-you-give-off-at-work-matters
8. https://psycnet.apa.org/record/2015-27503-001
9. https://hbr.org/2016/09/the-energy-you-give-off-at-work-matters

CHAPTER 5
1. https://hbr.org/2019/02/research-men-and-women-need-different-kinds
   -of-networks-to-succeed

CHAPTER 7
1. https://www.weforum.org/agenda/2016/05/3-ways-to-build-trust-in
   -your-business-05866831-1d47-4d4f-8b16-88ad8e0b7e59/
2. https://hbr.org/2020/01/research-how-to-build-trust-with-business
   -partners-from-other-cultures

CHAPTER 9
1. https://www.chicagotribune.com/entertainment/theater/ct-lois
   -weisberg-was-more-than-a-connector-ae-0117-20160114-column.html
2. https://hbr.org/2015/03/introverts-extroverts-and-the-complexities-of
   -team-dynamics
3. https://www.jstor.org/stable/3791464?seq=1
4. https://www.fastcompany.com/1809976/thou-shalt-covet-what-thy
   -neighbor-covets
5. http://www.ccnl.emory.edu/greg/Bernspercent20Conformitypercent20f
   inalpercent20printed.pdf

CHAPTER 10
1. https://email.uplers.com/blog/email-marketing-statistics/
2. https://www.lifewire.com/how-many-emails-are-sent-every-day
   -1171210
3. http://www-usr.rider.edu/~suler/psycyber/disinhibit.html
4. https://www.aspeninstitute.org/blog-posts/the-relationalist-manifesto/
5. https://www.aspeninstitute.org/programs/weave-the-social-fabric
   -initiative/

6. https://psycnet.apa.org/record/2005-16185-007
7. https://www.nytimes.com/2007/10/07/jobs/07pre.html
8. https://greatergood.berkeley.edu/article/item/the_four_keys_to _happiness_at_work
9. https://www.edx.org/professional-certificate/berkeleyx-science-of -happiness-at-work
10. https://greatergood.berkeley.edu/article/item/the_four_keys_to _happiness_at_work
11. https://greatergood.berkeley.edu/article/item/how_happy_are_people _at_work
12. https://www.ted.com/talks/professor_herminia_ibarra_the _authenticity_paradox
13. http://www.christineporath.com/books/
14. https://hiddentribes.us/pdf/hidden_tribes_report.pdf
15. https://www.ncbi.nlm.nih.gov/pmc/articles/PMC3603687/
16. https://pubmed.ncbi.nlm.nih.gov/15273013/
17. https://pubmed.ncbi.nlm.nih.gov/16737372/
18. https://hiddentribes.us/
19. https://hiddentribes.us/pdf/hidden_tribes_report.pdf
20. http://www.otheringandbelonging.org/the-problem-of-othering/
21. https://www.who.int/mental_health/evidence/burn-out/en/
22. https://www.forbes.com/sites/bryanrobinson/2019/12/08/two-thirds-of -workers-experienced-burnout-this-year-how-to-reverse-the-trend-in -2020/#711fb77974a0

CHAPTER 11

1. https://neuroleadership.com/personnel/david-rock/
2. https://conference.iste.org/uploads/ISTE2016/HANDOUTS/KEY _100525149/understandingtheSCARFmodel.pdf
3. https://conference.iste.org/uploads/ISTE2016/HANDOUTS/KEY _100525149/understandingtheSCARFmodel.pdf
4. https://hbswk.hbs.edu/item/ignore-this-advice-at-your-own-peril
5. https://www.inc.com/jessica-stillman/science-says-extremely-happy -people-all-share-this-conversation-style.html
6. https://onlinelibrary.wiley.com/doi/pdf/10.1111/comt.12106
7. https://www.fastcompany.com/3032550/what-happens-at-the-ultimate -summer-camp-for-influencers
8. https://www.nytimes.com/2015/01/11/style/36-questions-that-lead-to -love.html
9. https://ggia.berkeley.edu/practice/36_questions_for_increasing _closeness

10. https://hbr.org/2014/05/create-a-work-environment-that-fosters-flow

11. https://www.inc.com/betsy-mikel/how-brene-brown-runs-emotionally
-intelligent-zoom-meetings.html

12. https://www.theguardian.com/technology/2011/oct/09/steve-jobs
-stanford-commencement-address

13. https://greatergood.berkeley.edu/article/item/why_curious_people
_have_better_relationships#:~:text=

14. https://hbr.org/2018/09/curiosity

15. https://www.ncbi.nlm.nih.gov/pmc/articles/PMC3430822/

16. https://www.ncbi.nlm.nih.gov/pmc/articles/PMC3430822/

CHAPTER 12

1. https://pipelineangels.com/about-pipeline-angels/

2. https://www.sec.gov/spotlight/jobs-act.shtml

3. https://econsultancy.com/the-crowdfund-act-everything-you-need-to
-know/

4. https://www.bloomberg.com/company/stories/top-10-things-everyone
-know-women-consumers/

5. https://www.inc.com/dustin-mckissen/we-need-more-women-in
-venture-capital-heres-why-that-needs-to-change.html#:~:text=\

CHAPTER 13

1. https://journals.plos.org/plosone/article?id=10.1371/journal.pone
.0078433#:~:text=

2. https://www.washingtonpost.com/news/monkey-cage/wp/2017/02/07
/this-is-what-we-learned-by-counting-the-womens-marches/

INDEX

ABOUT THE AUTHOR

Susan McPherson is a serial connector, angel investor, and corporate responsibility expert. She is the founder and CEO of McPherson Strategies, a communications consultancy focused on the intersection of brands and social impact, providing storytelling, partnership creation, and visibility to corporations, NGOs, and social enterprises. She has over 25 years of experience in marketing, public relations, and sustainability communications. She speaks regularly at industry events including Inspirefest/Dublin, BSR, Center for Corporate Citizenship's Annual Summit, DLD, and Techonomy, and has contributed to the *Harvard Business Review*, *Fast Company*, and *Forbes*. She's appeared on *NPR* and *CNN*, as well as in *USA Today*, *The New Yorker*, *New York Magazine*, and the *Los Angeles Times*.

Currently, Susan invests in and advises women-led technology startups, including iFundWomen, Inc., Messy.fm, Our Place, The Riveter, Park Place Payments, Hint Water, Apolitical, Arlo Skye, Giapenta, and The Muse. She serves on the boards of USA for UNHCR, the 19th News, and the Lower Eastside Girls Club, and previously served on the board of Bpeace. Additionally, she is a member of the MIT Solve Women and Technology Leadership Group and serves as an adviser to several nonprofits, including Girls Who Code, Ocean Collective, She's the First, and The OpEd Project. Susan is a Vital Voices global corporate ambassador and has received numerous accolades for her voice on social media platforms from *Fortune Magazine*, *Fast Company*, and *Elle*. She resides in Brooklyn.

Visit: http://www.mcpstrategies.com.